EVERYONE'S GUIDE TO
ONLINE STOCK
MARKET INVESTING

Praise for...

Everyone's Guide to Online Stock Market Investing

'Alexander Davidson's skill is in presenting an enormous amount of fact and advice with such economy. Not a word is wasted. Every sentence hits its mark. The result is that in a couple of hundred pages he covers not only the basics of stock market investing, but also special areas like new issues, technical analysis, options, research on the Web, and penny shares, and he manages to tie them together in a coherent whole. This is a first-class book for anyone who wants to attain a broad understanding of how the markets work and to pick up important dos and don'ts from a seasoned investor along the way.'

Philip Jenks, Global-Investor.com Financial Bookshop

'A major new work for online investors. Online investing is here to stay and investors need to know the pros and cons. This book sets them out clearly and concisely. Buy it and read it!'

John Piper, Editor of The Technical Trader *and* Money Manager

'*Everyone's Guide to Online Stock Market Investing* offers novice and experienced investors a useful guide on using a vast array of Internet links and resources to improve investment performance and reduce costs.'

Jayesh Manek, Manek Investments

'While the Internet may have disappointed as an investment, it has not disappointed as an investment tool... This book should appeal to investors who consider themselves a novice in the online investment game as well as to those who are more experienced. It is highly readable and most of all practical, which is more than can be said for a lot of Web sites. There is more of a need for this book now than there was in the heady days in early 2000, because the sites left are the ones worth using... this book is an excellent guide to making the Internet work for you as an investor.'

Lawrence Gosling, Editor-in-Chief Investor's Week *and* Bloomberg Money *magazines.*

'Whether you made or lost money in the dot.com bubble, one thing is for sure – the Internet has revolutionized personal investing. The facilities, data, tools and services available to individual investors through the Internet are simply amazing – and they continue to grow more accessible and useable. Where you start, what you need to do, how to get free data, which are the useful Web sites to look at, the best tools to use... all this and its comprehensive Web site listings make *Everyone's Guide to Online Stock Market Investing* the ideal starting point for investors wanting to extract the maximum value from the Internet.'

Chris Gilchrist, Editor of investment newsletter The IRS Report

EVERYONE'S GUIDE TO ONLINE STOCK MARKET INVESTING

The Definitive 12-DAY Guide

Alexander Davidson

KOGAN PAGE

*To my past and future clients,
this book is for you*

First published in 2002

Apart from any fair dealing for the purposes of research or private study, or criticism or review, as permitted under the Copyright, Designs and Patents Act 1988, this publication may only be reproduced, stored or transmitted, in any form or by any means, with the prior permission in writing of the publishers, or in the case of reprographic reproduction in accordance with the terms and licences issued by the CLA. Enquiries concerning reproduction outside these terms should be sent to the publishers at the undermentioned address:

Kogan Page Limited
120 Pentonville Road
London N1 9JN
UK

© Alexander Davidson, 2002

The right of Alexander Davidson to be identified as the author of this work has been asserted by him in accordance with the Copyright, Designs and Patents Act 1988.

British Library Cataloguing in Publication Data

A CIP record for this book is available from the British Library.

ISBN 0 7494 3643 3

Typeset by JS Typesetting, Wellingborough, Northants
Printed and bound in Great Britain by Clays Ltd, St Ives plc

Contents

	Acknowledgements	*vii*
	Introduction	**1**
Day 1	The stock market online	3
Day 2	How to choose and use an online broker	19
Day 3	Become your own online equities analyst	37
Day 4	How to win as a share trader	59
Day 5	How technical analysis can make you money	73
Day 6	How to win in the penny share casino	91
Day 7	How to make a killing on new issues	109
Day 8	Secrets of stock tipsters	123
Day 9	How to profit from traded options and warrants	133
Day 10	The daredevil trader: financial futures, spread betting, CFDs and forex	147
Day 11	Alternatives to online dealing	159
Day 12	Rich dividends from reading	171
	A final word	183
	Appendix	*185*
	Index	*211*

By the same author:

How to Win in a Volatile Stock Market

How to Win in a Volatile Stock Market focuses on tested strategies for selecting and buying undervalued shares and other assets at rock-bottom prices and commissions. City professionals are making fortunes by applying these simple but little-known investment techniques. In this book, the rules of the game are set down in an easy-to-read style by a former City share-dealer with first-hand experience.

The author, Alexander Davidson, introduces his Bargain Hunters' Investment FlexiSystem, which shows you how to:

- select and invest in dynamic small-company stocks overlooked by the market;
- find the few Internet stocks that could soar in value as the rest founder;
- hand-pick the blue chips likely to rise the most;
- make a potential killing interpreting market trends and financial news flow;
- discover the hidden meaning of company accounts;
- balance your stocks effectively between sectors.

In addition, there is advice on how to harness the immense investment resources of the Internet, including buying and selling shares online. The secrets of *successful* day-trading are revealed. US and European markets are featured, and the entire spectrum of financial services comes under scrutiny.

How to Win in a Volatile Stock Market gives even the most cautious and inexperienced private investors a workable blueprint for making money. If you only read one book on investing this year, this has to be it.

Available from all good bookshops. To obtain further information, please contact the publisher at the address below:

Kogan Page Ltd
120 Pentonville Road
London N1 9JN
Tel: 020 7278 0433
Fax: 020 7837 6348
www.kogan-page.co.uk

Acknowledgements

Thanks to Jon Finch for his great enthusiasm and skill in commissioning and editing this book. Thanks too to Martha Fumagalli for helping to get the project going.

A special thanks to Natasha Roschina in St Petersburg for her fantastic Web site design and so much more.

My thanks to the IFR equities team, Victoria, Helen, Mark, Paul and Sheila, for days on end filled with fun and inspiration.

Thanks to friends, colleagues and contacts in the stockbroking and investment banking community who have been so ready to help.

The investment methods described in this book have worked exceptionally well for some investors in the past in both good and bad market conditions, but may not suit everybody all of the time. This book is for educational purposes only, and in no way offers specific investment advice. Also the author has made every effort to include up-to-date Web site addresses and information in this book, but things change, particularly in volatile stock markets. Any investments that you make are of your own choice and at your own risk.

Introduction

What this book is about

In this small book, I will show you proven ways to make money from online investing on the stock market, which you can then adapt for your own purposes. You will find the material presented logically in the form of an easy-to-read course.

Investing in shares online, if you get it right, is not just lucrative but is fun as well. This can apply when stock markets are down. In this book, you will find guidance for investing in *all* market conditions. The course is ideal for beginners, but also has much to offer the more experienced investor.

Become an online investor in 12 days

Time is short, and this book is designed to be read in 12 days. The information is presented in modules entitled Day, 1 Day 2 etc and I suggest that you read one module a day. The modules will take you through from the basics of online investing to far beyond. You can master online investing *on top of your full time job or other commitments*. This is important. Most people cannot just put down all their other commitments to concentrate on investing.

To make the learning process easier, the modules are broken down into succinct sections under separate headings, so that you can digest the material in bite-size chunks – on the train, in the bath, in bed, and while waiting at the bus stop. It will be helpful if, at some point, you have access to the Internet so that you can look up Web sites referred to. But even this is not essential at this stage.

The modules are to some extent interlinked, and are parts of the whole. I therefore recommend that you do not make any new investments until you have completed all 12 modules.

Your approach

Use a highlighter pen to emphasize points that seem important, so it will be easy for you to go back to them. This book is a tool through which you may get started, and improve your skills, in online investing. It is not a leather-bound first edition that you hardly dare touch for fear of damaging. *You must make this material your own.*

In so doing, do not expect an easy ride. But if you put an effort into learning, by the time you have finished, you will have a sound grasp of ratio analysis, discounted cash flow analysis, reading the charts, choosing your broker, the mechanics of buying and selling shares, new issues and a whole lot more.

You will also find that this book guides you towards *thinking like a successful investor*, which is far more important than cramming investment facts or – worse still – learning mainly about the technology. At the end of each module there is a summary of important points covered.

Time to put your books away

Once you have read this book, you should be ready to invest with confidence. Be prepared to make some mistakes at first, and take responsibility for these. Although I am giving you all the help that I can, any investment is ultimately your own choice – and at your own risk.

That is the preliminaries over. Now hold onto your hat, dear reader, as I am going to take you on the most thrilling journey of your life, the roller coaster ride of online stock market investing.

The author invites you to visit his Web site at www.flexinvest.co.uk and to contact him by e-mail through this route.

Day 1
The stock market online

Overview

The Internet is the best thing that ever happened for you as a private investor in the stock market. It gives you more information about products and services than was ever available before it existed, and it provides efficient facilities for investing. When used properly, it makes investing a far less stressful experience than it used to be.

In this module, we will look at the basics of investing online using the unique Online Share Buyer's FlexiSystem. We will see how the system evolved, and the related benefits of buying shares for value, even if they are unpopular.

We will critically examine the role of analysts, and explore the world of investment clubs. You will find here an introduction to two popular beginners' investment Web sites, and we will touch on investing abroad.

The paper-free revolution

For those who hate being deluged with paperwork, the Internet offers a glorious freedom. You can browse at length, using a search engine to quickly sort out the most relevant sites, and you can read strictly on screen. You can print off hard copies selectively.

If you want to use an online broker, you will still usually have to print off a form which you must sign and post. But the form will be instantly available to you. The days of having to telephone the firm to ask for a form then await its arrival in the post are over.

Online brokers are increasingly packing everything into their user-friendly Web sites. On the best of these you can not only buy and sell shares, obtain real time quotes and track your portfolio, but you will have access to invaluable analysis and financial news flow. You can apply value filters in selecting stocks, and the computer will automatically find the companies within your range.

In addition, there is a huge variety of independent Web sites that can help you as an investor. Some offer multimedia presentations, including slide shows and video interviews with chief executives. Through online message boards, you can discuss stocks with others and receive instant feedback.

Internet on the move

You can access the Internet and, in many cases, your broker's account, from your computer anywhere in the world. In addition, some online services are available via WAP (wireless application protocol) mobile phones and handheld devices. As yet, these services are limited, but the potential is vast. We will be taking a peek at these on Day 2.

Real human contact is missing

The flip side to online stock market investing – and the research that goes with it – is that real human contact is often missing. If you are the type of person who needs your hand held while making your investment decisions, or needs somebody else to make them for you, you will prefer telephone or face-to-face contact. The Internet will not be enough, but it will still be very useful.

All sites are not equal

The other problem with online investing is that so much of the information available is of no value to you. This book will show you how to bypass the less useful sites – perhaps selling services that you do not need, or providing out-of-date news flow – and to focus on those that can really help you.

A proven method of value investing

The legendary Bargain Hunters' Investment FlexiSystem

The aggregate of investment techniques covered in this book is exclusive. It has its roots in the very successful Bargain Hunters' Investment FlexiSystem, which I describe in detail in my best-selling book *How to Win in a Volatile Stock Market*.

Let me give you some background. The Bargain Hunters' Investment FlexiSystem came into use a few years ago at some major City investment banks. Using the FlexiSystem, some friends and colleagues who work there – a select band of City traders, salespeople, analysts and others – have quietly made money on the stock markets in good times and in bad.

At its most basic, the FlexiSystem involves buying undervalued stocks cheaply, and waiting until they rise substantially before selling out. But there are various ways to tackle the job and flexibility is the key word. The magazine *Shares* said accurately of the FlexiSystem that it 'starts with value investing, stirs in some growth techniques, and adds a healthy dollop of common sense'.

The FlexiSystem works because there are value anomalies on the stock market. Some stocks are bargains and others are not. This gives the lie to the Random Walk theory, which suggests that if you select stocks at random, they will perform at least as well on average as those picked on value criteria.

The Random Walk theory is a strong version of the efficient market hypothesis, which suggests that all known or knowable news is discounted in the share price. Some academics still love it. In the real world, it does not work. The overwhelming evidence is that skilled investors – including those using our system properly – more often than not make superior returns.

Internet stockbrokers are ideal

Users of our FlexiSystem prefer to use execution-only brokers. These offer low-commission dealing because they carry out transactions without offering expensive back-up advisory services. The cheapest and most efficient brokers in this category are now Internet brokers.

These have gradually become the number one choice for almost all serious users of our system in its current form.

The Online Share Buyer's FlexiSystem

In keeping with this trend, the Bargain Hunters' Investment FlexiSystem has evolved into an online version. It retains its roots in value investing, but requires better information access, and speed of execution, both of which are enhanced online. It places more emphasis on trading than before, and gives charting more credence, at least for providing a snapshot picture of a stock's or index's prowess. Today's users of the FlexiSystem now commonly invest in continental Europe and the United States, as well as in the UK.

Users of the Online Share Buyer's FlexiSystem – as the new version is known – already have a pension, life assurance, and rainy day money – perhaps £5,000 stashed in the highest interest account that they can find. They may also have some unit trusts (typically tracker funds, which by tracking a stock market index outperform most other unit trusts on a net basis, partly due to their low charges) or investment trusts.

They will have bought some financial products through discount brokers, which typically offer you more for your money because they charge less commission in exchange for not giving you any personalized financial advice. See the Appendix (page 192) for a list of discount brokers.

With these staple investments in place, users of the Online Share Buyer's FlexiSystem are focusing almost exclusively on investing in shares. Partly because so many of them are, or have been, City professionals, they are far more successful at the game than most.

These canny investors do not get swept up in crowd hysteria. They know to buy when the markets have hit rock-bottom and shares are going cheap. Conversely, they save their money when the bull market has soared too far and less sophisticated investors are piling into shares. This book will show you how to take a similar contrary approach.

Buy low, sell high

The Online Share Buyer's FlexiSystem involves, above all, buying shares that are under-priced compared with the company's underlying fundamental value. Over time – although not necessarily in the short term – investors will rush to buy the bargain stock, sending the share price up to a realistic level and beyond. At this point, it may be wise to sell out.

Fair enough, I hear you saying, but do not all investors try to buy a stock cheaply and sell when it is overpriced? Paradoxically, they do not. Let me demonstrate this by turning back the clocks. In late 1999 and early 2000, the bull market in the UK and continental Europe, led by the US market, was at a height. Private and institutional investors were rushing to buy telecommunications, media and technology (TMT) stocks, which were soaring in value.

From March 2000, the market underwent a massive correction. These investors made money – in some cases quite a lot of it – if they cashed in their paper profits on TMT stocks on the cusp of the downturn, or just before it happened.

In practice, some institutions did not bear the brunt of the market reversal. They had offloaded plenty of TMT stocks in time. They are used to buying and selling very quickly to meet short-term price targets. Private investors are neither so quick to sell nor so confident about it. Many were left holding stocks that were rapidly dwindling in value.

Some of these investors were speculators and not investors. The late Benjamin Graham, famous as the grandfather of value investing, made a point of distinguishing between the two categories. So what is the difference?

The lemming effect

If you speculate on shares, you will be making your buying and selling decisions on price movements. You will rush to buy a favoured hot stock whose price is soaring for no rational reason. This reflects copycat buying by unthinking investors. Most will almost certainly not have made any attempt to value the stock that they are chasing.

So long as many investors rush to buy the stock, its price will keep rising. It will either be overvalued against fundamentals, or will become so. The problem is that investors are notoriously fickle. At the slightest excuse, or none, they will rush to sell, sending the over-inflated share price plummeting.

In the year following March 2000, some inflated TMT stocks fell in value by 50 per cent or more within hours. Over a longer period since, some have fallen by 90 per cent or more. Investors who had bought into such stocks at their peak and who got out too late, if at all, saw their capital decimated. It is easy to be wise after the event.

Users of the Online Share Buyer's FlexiSystem, however, *never got caught in the first place*. They buy stocks at a price which represents value and they are prepared to hold them. This is investing, not speculating. More specifically, it is a form of value investing.

Since the stock market correction from late March 2000, interest in the Online Share Buyer's FlexiSystem has spiralled. This is logical. When markets are down, value investing always comes into fashion. But if you are a *true* value investor, you will always apply the same stock-picking principles regardless of whether markets are up or down.

Take a leaf out of the book of Mark Slater, a highly successful fund manager and son of famous UK stock market guru Jim Slater. He told me that he avoids watching the screens for day-by-day news flow and economic indicators as he does not want to be influenced in his stock-picking decisions by such 'noise'. This is an extreme tactic since news items can be significant, but it demonstrates the principle that, if you are buying a stock for value, what happens in the market as a whole should not be too relevant.

Online investing encourages speculation

As we have seen, most investors are heavily influenced by the market. They buy when the market is high, and investment euphoria is strong. They do nothing when the market is low. They are speculating on price movements rather than buying for value, but are getting their timing wrong.

Professionals with vested interests will hate me for saying this, but online stockbroking encourages such speculation. Anybody who has sufficient funds and access to the Internet can open an online account, and buy and sell shares. You need simply sit in front of your computer and tap the right keys.

This, coupled with the sheer quantity of financial information thrust at you – including, in many cases, from the broker's Web site – contributes to the illusion that online investing is an easy way to make money. It is not.

Assess a company for value

With the help of this book, you will soon be investing online in a more rigorous way than the vast majority of investors. From Day 3, which is about fundamental valuation, you will learn how to assess whether a company looks cheap or not. Once you have valued the company in this way, you need to assess whether the market is likely to recognize and close the gap between value and price within a reasonable time period. If so, you will buy the shares. The gap is more likely to be closed if the underlying company has strong management, growth prospects, and is making a bigger return on its capital than the amount it pays for it. To assess the company's value, you will need some understanding of company accounts.

Get to grips with company accounts

After reading this book, you will understand the basics of ratio analysis, which is how to assess a company based on the numbers culled from its report and accounts. A company's cash position is crucial, as cash cannot be manipulated while profits can. On Day 3, I will explain how to discount future cash flows to a present day value. This valuation technique, although unreliable, is the one that investment analysts use most widely.

Self-evidently, discounted cash-flow analysis is more suitable for companies with predictable cash flows. This excludes most young high-tech and Internet companies. Billionaire value investor Warren Buffett has declined investment in such companies. Pundits sneered at this tactic during late 1999, but by mid-2000 when high-tech stocks collapsed, his position was thoroughly vindicated.

Timing matters

If a stock is good value in relation to the share price, it is theoretically the right time to buy. In practice, if the stock is plummeting in price – regardless of value – it may be better to wait until it has reached rock bottom before you commit your money.

It is psychologically hard to buy a share when it has fallen sharply in price. This is because nobody else is buying. But this is when the gap between price and value may be largest. As a successful value investor, using our FlexiSystem, you will often be investing against popular opinion.

Users of the Online Share Buyer's FlexiSystem view holding shares as part ownership in a business. They are prepared to hold shares for at least three to four years, and will sell only when the share price no longer offers value. Sometimes they will *trade* shares for the short term as well, but only with money that they can afford to lose. In this area, different rules of the FlexiSystem apply. See Day 4 for further details.

Establish your circle of competence

As a medium- to long-term investor, you should establish your circle of competence and invest only in businesses that you understand. Be wary of companies that are growing very rapidly without creating value for shareholders. Stock market analysts may recommend buying such companies entirely on future prospects. Their valuations may be 'pie in the sky'.

In 1999 and early 2000, when Internet company investment mania was at its peak, almost all Internet analysts were putting *buy* recommendations on companies that the stock market had ludicrously overvalued. They used all sorts of innovative valuation methods, including price as a percentage of eyeballs on the Web site, or of subscriber numbers. Some of these methods have been largely discredited.

Method in their madness

These analysts had method in their madness. In many cases, they had – or were angling for – the Internet companies that they were analysing as corporate clients. In this context, particularly in bull markets, analysts are paid not for giving objective opinions on stocks, but for drumming up corporate business. They are glorified salespeople, a far cry from their hole-in-the-corner role of 20 years ago when they scrutinized the report and accounts and tried to offer an unbiased valuation.

Impartiality is also affected in that the analysts are highly dependent on the company that they are analysing to feed them information. If an analyst upsets the company, it may 'blank' him or her in the future, which could jeopardize his or her career. An analyst will rarely issue a *sell* recommendation on a company.

Analysts are more likely to issue a long-term *hold* or *reduce* recommendation, which is a disguised way of saying the same thing – and even this only after the stock has declined in value. They will reveal their true feelings about the company only in discreet conversation with favoured clients.

If analysts pass on price-sensitive information that is not generally known, they could be guilty of insider trading. In practice, this goes on sometimes, but the parties involved are discreet. Otherwise, the company manages its information flow. This is why analysts often release similar profit forecasts and perspectives on a company. The less discerning take what the company tells them at face value.

Analysts are not corrupt

Although they often face a conflict of interests, investment analysts are not corrupt as the media has been known to represent them. They are merely playing a complicated game, in which institutional investors and companies are also players. All these big players know the rules – written and unwritten – and can look after their interests.

These interests do not always coincide with your own. The research that most investment analysts produce is not meant for you. Your capital for investing, time frame, and investment priorities will differ from those of the institutions. Be cautious.

Diversification

When you start investing, diversify your portfolio. This means that you should invest in a range of sectors. It is safest to have the bulk of your shares in the 100 largest companies that make up the FTSE-100 index. The sheer size of these companies – as measured by market capitalization, (share price x number of shares in issue) makes them safer investments than most. However, the safety net of size is no longer as strong as it was. Some high-tech stocks in the FTSE-100 such as Sage, the accounting software group, and ARM Holdings, the computer chip licensor, have fallen drastically in value since early 2000.

A diversified portfolio invested in the FTSE-100 companies might include such racy stocks – perhaps ARM Holdings and Vodafone, the mobile phone giant. On the more cautious side, it might include a bank such as HSBC and Rolls Royce, the car maker.

You could also diversify out of the FTSE-100, by including some smaller companies. Do not hold all your money in equities. Consider putting some of your cash into gilts, which are bonds 100 per cent secured by the British government, or in corporate bonds. Always keep a small amount in your building society for emergencies.

Diversification, then, is a good idea – but in moderation. Diversification reduces risk, but it also reduces reward by diluting gains from your best stocks. It can be too much of a good thing. Once you have become an old hand at the Online Share Buyer's FlexiSystem, you will see that it is better to pick five good stocks and put all your money into these, than to go for ten stocks, of which some are mediocre, and maybe one or two bad. In your early days as an investor, another way to find safety in numbers is to invest as part of an investment club.

Investment clubs

Investment clubs, where people combine resources and skills for investing in shares, are a mixed blessing. They serve a useful purpose in that they encourage investors to invest, and take loneliness out of the process. Even if the club loses money, the losses may not be great after they have been distributed over the group. Some online brokers astutely encourage investment clubs to place their business with them.

Of course, an investment club, like any activity group, can fail. A good analogy may be found in creative writing groups. Before I was first published as a novelist, I joined a few of these. The problem often was that would-be writers involved all had different ideas about their craft. Some were simply hobbyists looking to express their feelings. Others used writing as a therapy, and came out with disturbing stuff. A few were more serious, but the quality of their output varied, and often had no correlation with their perception of it. There were often misunderstandings and conflicts.

No less of a mismatch can occur in investment clubs. Members can usefully pool different levels of know-how and life experience, but *only* if they share the same broad view on how to invest. In practice, this sometimes does not happen. For instance, short-term traders (see Day 4), and technical analysts (see Day 5) have a very different strategy from value investors. People in their 20s are usually less risk averse than those in their 60s, but are also more foolhardy.

Despite the potential problems, many investment clubs operate in harmony. At this stage, you will find it hard to track down a group that focuses seriously on investing in the style of the Online Share Buyer's FlexiSystem. Usually investment clubs focus on buying what is fashionable, and this can be disastrous unless you adopt the short-term trader's discipline, and the commitment that goes with this.

If you want to be part of an investment club but cannot find one that is implementing the Online Share Buyer's FlexiSystem, consider setting up your own. In the UK, this is easier than you might think. First visit the Web site of Proshare, the body that promotes wider share ownership (www.proshare.org). Online, you can buy its famous investment club start-up manual, which provides simple-to-follow instructions that have stood the test of time.

You will run your club most easily as a partnership with a legal maximum of 20 members. In their number, you will need a treasurer, who issues monthly financial statements, as well as a chairman and secretary. Members will contribute a regular subscription – perhaps £30 a month – to the club's investment fund, and will be entitled to give notice and sell out, removing their stake at its current value. You could hold meetings monthly, ideally in a neutral location such as a pub.

When making your investment decisions – alone, or as part of the group – make full use of Internet resources. I refer to some of the best throughout this book, and in a full list in the appendix. At this early stage, I will alert you to my two favourite beginners' Web sites. If you explore these for yourself, it will be time well spent.

Resources at your disposal

The Motley Fool UK Web site

First check out the Motley Fool UK Web site (www.fool.co.uk). This is run by self-styled Fools (with a large F) in the Shakespearean sense, who tell the king the truth when others merely flatter him. In this case, they are speaking to investors about the stock market and other areas of the financial services industry.

These Fools are critical of the Wise, which is their sarcastic umbrella term for commission-hungry financial services professionals. The Wise are represented as exploiting the ignorance of investors to sell them unsuitable products wrapped in unnecessary mystique. If you too have Foolish tendencies, you can register with the site and communicate your thoughts to like-minded Fools via the site's electronic message boards.

The Motley Fool UK Web site provides daily market updates, idiosyncratic stock analysis and educational features. The Fools run several mock share portfolios on an ongoing basis and share buying and selling decisions with their online community. As the chief UK Fool has admitted to me, the standard of writing is not always professional. However, this fits with the Motley Fool's message: the man in the street can beat the Wise investment professionals at their own game.

Get to know this Web site. Read, learn and be entertained. Explore and contribute to the fantastic message boards. The site is particularly good at explaining simply how technology companies work. But do not rush to invest in the style of the site's model portfolios. In this area, the Motley Fool has had some successes but also made some disastrous mistakes. I hate to say it, but sometimes 'Fools rush in where angels fear to tread'.

Ample

For a more straight-laced approach, try the Ample (www.ample.com) Web site owned by AMP Group, the international financial service company that has taken over Interactive Investor International. As this book goes to press, Ample has merged Interactive Investor's Web site with its own. Ample plans to keep and, in some cases, enhance the original equities-related services of the Interactive Investor Web site. These include news updates, stock recommendations, a technical analysis commentary, and a large variety of extra features. You may still set up a portfolio online that shows updated share prices, and participate in message boards. In the first quarter of 2002, Ample plans to add facilities for buying ISAs, and for online dealing.

We will look further at using message boards later in this book. This interactive element of Internet usage can be valuable, but is open to manipulation. For this reason, be sceptical. Of course, the more you learn about the stock market, the less likely you are to fall prey to rogue suggestions. Reading this book will take you a long way, but why not take advantage of online investment education as well?

Online investment education

Recently, a variety of investment courses have surfaced on the Internet. These will guide you through the basics, sometimes to an advanced level. The best of this education is independent. The worst sites provide only a thinly disguised sales pitch for their expensive trading seminars, online newsletters or charting software.

Even some of the better investment courses can be hard to download. For access, you may need Adobe Acrobat which, if you are an unseasoned Internet user, can create a hurdle. Some courses are free, while others have a credit system that charges per number of units used. Some of the beginners' courses available are patronizingly oversimplified.

Let me tell you about my favourite Web site for free stock market education. This is Stock Academy (www.stockacademy.com), an online broker. Its courses are easy to read, succinct and well prepared. Each module has a quiz to test what you have learnt, and a valuable reading list.

Survival of the fittest

Once you have started using the Internet as an investor, you will wonder how you ever managed without it. But in your forays online, be cautious. Many financial Web sites are not receiving enough advertising revenue to fund marketing expenditure, and users are loathe to pay subscriptions unless the service is exceptional. In late 2000, one journalistically excellent UK financial Web site, thestreet.co.uk, a subsidiary of the excellent US-based thestreet.com, ceased trading in the UK, and many City professionals mourned its loss. Other sites are likely to follow suit.

Of those financial Web sites that have pulled through, some have been bought up by larger players, while others have struck up deals with online brokers. Many supplement their income by selling courses, books and other services, on either a proprietary or an agency basis. Some focus on UK investing, while others have broadened their coverage to continental Europe, the United States and beyond.

Invest abroad

Initial considerations

Access to the various Web sites gives you every opportunity to expand your investment horizons. Consider investing abroad, but only after you have gained some UK investing experience.

To proceed, you will need to consider the exchange rate, as well as the share price. Also look at dealing costs, which are falling sharply for continental Europe and the United States, but which can still be high through some brokers.

Generally, European stock markets swing in tandem. The benefits from investing in French, German or Swedish stocks are not necessarily very different from benefits of investing in UK stocks. The biggest influence on Europe comes from the United States, which takes a lead. You can now invest directly in the United States market through some UK online brokers, as well as through US firms (see Day 2).

Emerging markets

If you want to be really adventurous, consider investing in emerging markets. The two largest are Poland, which has a flourishing stock exchange, and Russia. Other Eastern European countries such as Hungary and the Czech Republic have, at the time of writing, much more limited investment opportunities.

Of course, emerging markets are risky. Before investing, you will need to dig a little, and to form an opinion of sectors, stocks and economies in a local as well as global context. You must at all costs avoid getting caught up in the wrong stocks or markets.

In your endeavours, the Internet, if used to its full extent, will probably be of enormous assistance. Through a search engine such as Excite (www.excite.co.uk), you can gain access to stock research, market reports, stock exchange profiles, and similar information about all the major (and plenty of minor) regions in the world. The Appendix gives a list of useful Web sites that includes some foreign stock exchanges.

As you surf in this way, you will be at an advantage if you have a reading knowledge of a relevant foreign language. You can develop this without leaving your computer. Let me tell you about my friend Peter who, in early 2001, became interested in buying Russian equities. Russia had recently emerged from its 1998 financial crisis and it was possible to buy locally quoted stocks at rock-bottom prices. Stocks were typically priced 85 per cent lower than their sector peers in Western Europe and the United States. This reflected that the companies had not resolved corporate governance issues, including clarity of accounting.

Peter found some useful Web sites that advised in English on investing in Russia. One of these was Dover Capital (www.dover-capital.com). However, many important sites were presented only in Russian. Bravely, Peter tackled the task of learning Russian from resources available free on the Internet. Within weeks, he had achieved enough knowledge to be able to read Russian Web sites with the help of a dictionary. You can do the same for your chosen country.

American depositary receipts (ADRs)

Some markets outside Europe are so illiquid that, if you buy shares, you cannot easily sell out. If you make a complaint about how the deal was handled, you will as a foreign investor receive little priority. Court cases can be almost impossible to conduct abroad.

The easiest way round such risks is often to buy American depositary receipts (ADRs). These are US domestic securities representing ownership of a foreign stock, and are available through brokers who deal in US shares.

ADRs work out slightly more expensive than the underlying securities, but are liquid. They give you access to proper reporting information about the company and fast news flow. You will be notified of dividends and structural reorganizations, which is not invariably the case when you invest directly on the home markets. To find out more about ADRs, I recommend you visit the highly informative ADR Web site of US investment bank JP Morgan (www.adr.com).

The way forward

The Online Share Buyer's FlexiSystem is not for everybody. If you are going to use it, you will need patience and independence of spirit. You can, in fact, learn these qualities. Read on and you may find yourself better prepared for investing in the stock market than you ever imagined.

Dynamic rules of the Online Share Buyer's FlexiSystem

- Use the Internet selectively to help with your stock market investment decisions.
- Do not chase price movements in shares but, instead, look to buy value.
- Get to grips with company accounts.
- Use online-brokers for a fast, cheap service.
- As an investor, be prepared to hold stocks for at least three to four years (except when trading).
- Treat analysts' recommendations with caution. They are likely to be aimed at institutional investors, who have different priorities from you.
- Invest in businesses that you understand.
- Diversify your portfolio, but in moderation.
- Consider joining a suitable investment club, or starting up your own.
- Explore two fantastic beginners' Web sites: the Motley Fool UK (www.fool.co.uk) and Ample (www.ample.com).
- Use free investment education sources on the Web, particularly at Stock Academy (www.stockacademy.com).
- Consider investing abroad, using the Internet for research purposes.

Day 2
How to choose and use an online broker

Overview

The hurdle that most investors face is whether to take the online investing route in the first place. Once you understand the advantages, you will have every incentive to master the practicalities.

In this module, we will look at the benefits of dealing online. You will learn how to select the broker that suits your needs, using our unique checklist. We will examine the practicalities of opening an account, dealing and settlement.

We will finally look at some issues with which you are faced as a shareholder, including dividends, rights issues and tax matters. You will discover how to make effective complaints about incompetent or dubious service. (See also Day 11, where we discuss using an advisory broker.)

Why use an online dealer?

If you buy and sell shares online, you are in most cases dealing with an execution-only stockbroker, which simply executes your trade without giving advice on it. This way, you will be taking charge of your own financial destiny – but the onus is on you to make the right investment decisions.

The online brokers have four practical advantages:

- They are cheap – because they will deal at low commissions. They can do this because they have limited staff costs, and high volumes of trade. When you are ready to invest, find a broker that charges the lowest commissions compatible with a good quality of service. Do not be enticed by a cash-back offer or similar on your first deal, if the broker offering this is not otherwise the best for you.
- They are accessible to some extent at all times. Although the range of information and services offered by online brokers varies, you can visit your broker's Web site 24 hours per day. You should always have access to your portfolio, with up-to-date share prices. You will often be able to pull up charts showing price movements of selected stocks or indices.
- They offer a fast service. Some online brokers are slower than others. But they all probably offer a faster dealing service than you would receive from your traditional broker if you were hanging on the phone in a busy period trying to get hold of him or her. Through some firms you can place deals after trading hours, and they will be executed when the market opens the next morning. We will examine this facility in more detail in the next module.
- They will deal in very small sizes. This is useful particularly when you are starting out as an investor.

Which online broker is best for you? You can choose from many in the UK, or broaden your search to continental Europe and the United States. The brokers operate with varying levels of service, and with different cost structures, but are essentially competing on price. We will now look at the five main categories of online broker.

Glorified e-mail services

Some brokers simply offer you the opportunity to issue buy or sell instructions by e-mail, rather than by ordinary mail or by making a phone call. Before mid-1998, a number of brokers operated like this. It is no longer the most efficient way. Use such a broker only if you deal infrequently, in stocks whose prices tend not to have much intra-day fluctuation.

Browser-based brokers

The majority of online brokers – led by Charles Schwab – are browser-based. These brokers allow you to execute a trade yourself, rather than asking the broker to do it for you. You can deal at a price shown on screen through a connection with computers at the London Stock Exchange.

When Internet traffic is heavy, you may find it a slow process to obtain quotes and stock charts from a browser-based broker's Web site, and to execute deals. This is because of the convoluted process for retrieving data. Your data request must pass from the computer, via the Internet, to the broker's server. The server will reconstruct the broker's Web page to include the updated data, before it becomes available on your computer via the Internet. An intermediary is often involved.

Some brokers will give you a price for only one stock at a time, so you cannot see this against the simultaneous price movements of other stocks. Unusually, Stocktrade.co.uk, the online broker that is part of Brewin Dolphin, offers free live streaming (updated) prices.

Alternatively, you will find free access to real-time share prices at the Web site of LondonMoneyMarket.com (www.Londonmoneymarket.com). Here you can also watch stock market indices as they change, and will have access to charts. You can also obtain real-time share prices from an independent market data subscription service such as that provided by Thomson Financial Network incorporating marketeye.com (www.thomsonfn.com).

Active trader brokers

Active trader brokers offer more efficient service than their browser-based cousins. They provide software to load onto your computer, which will evaluate your portfolio, construct charts, and enable fast trade execution. This way, you can deal on up-to-date information. The firms will not delay execution by asking for order confirmation, as some browser-based brokers do.

There is a halfway house. Some firms offer active trader facilities to their more active clients. For example, E*Trade UK offers Power Trade online software to those who make at least 30 trades a quarter. This provides streaming news and equity prices, and advanced charting. The screen shows who bought what stocks, at what prices.

Active trader facilities can seem expensive but, by enabling you to deal faster, can save you a fortune in the long run.

Level 11 data

Level 11 data is available through active trader brokers, but also independently. This is for serious investors and traders. It gives you the full range of bid-offer spreads from the market makers, who quote prices to your broker on a wholesale basis. The spread is the difference between the bid price (at which you can sell) or the offer price (at which you can buy). Let us suppose that a spread is 130–136. The lower figure of 130 is the bid price, while 136 is the offer price.

Level 11 data shows you when a market maker has changed its spread. It also provides transaction logs, which contain an updated record of trades filled. Through these, you can see the level of demand for a stock beyond the best bid and ask prices, which will show you how much resistance there is to price changes.

Advisory brokers operating online

If you buy and sell shares online, you must normally reckon to do without a broker's advice. At the time of writing, only one broker offers online dealing combined with a telephone advisory service, although a number offer both facilities separately.

Broking on-the-move

If you want stock market news and dealing facilities on-the-move, you need access to the mobile Internet. This is at present much more limited than the Web but, 3G, the latest wireless data transmission system, will make mobile dealing much easier.

To obtain access to the mobile Internet, you will need a suitable WAP mobile phone or PDA (personal digital assistant) such as a Psion.

On the mobile Internet, you will have access to such sites as Digital Look (www.digitallook.com), which has news, analysts' quotes and forecasts. Also available is FT.com (www.ft.com), which offers news, some analysis, and share price quotes. You can obtain alerts on share price movements relevant to your portfolio from Web sites such as Stock Alerts (www.stockalerts.com) or Sharepeople (www.sharepeople.com).

Brokers are increasingly offering a facility to trade online realtime from a WAP phone. One of the leaders in the field is T D Waterhouse's MobileBroker service (www.tdwaterhouse.co.uk). By 2004, nine out of ten mobile phones are expected to have WAP capacity.

Now we have seen the range of online brokers available, we will look at why you might choose one rather than another in your chosen category. Do not be loyal to any broker, as you will not be rewarded for it. Go for the deal that suits you best at any given time. Let us take a look at the services that brokers provide.

Online broker checklist

The basics

All brokers will provide trading facilities and some sort of on-site information and instructions. At any time you can view details of your account online, including current portfolio, trading history, and cash or stock transfers. The quality of these services will vary.

Back-up services

Sometimes you cannot get access to a site due to system failure, or when the broker is upgrading the site. Check whether your broker offers a telephone dealing service as a back-up. In any case, note the broker's telephone number.

Also, open an account with another broker as a back-up. You can use this back-up account more easily for buying than selling shares. If your shares are held electronically with one broker, to sell them through another would involve the transfer of your nominee holdings. This is an expensive hassle.

The issue will not arise if you hold share certificates – the old-fashioned and increasingly rare paper alternative to nominee holdings. We will return to this subject shortly under the heading of Settlement (p29).

Investor security

In the past, brokers have experienced security problems. At the end of 1999, one online broker had a security failure, and clients could gain access to each other's accounts. To avoid this kind of risk, brokers use encryption. This makes sure that the information passed between you and the broker online is scrambled. You can only make sense of the information by using the right encryption software, and an individual key code. Check that your broker uses 128-bit encryption, which is the strongest kind, and this aspect of security should not worry you.

Make sure also that your broker has insurance in place to protect client accounts in case it should run into financial problems.

Your broker will have issued you with a password of your choice. Make it a nonsense word, using letters as well as numbers, and keep it secret. Do not leave your computer on when you are in the secure part of your broker's Web site, and do not let people watch over your shoulder. When you have completed a transaction, make sure that you log out correctly.

Dealing costs

For some useful comparisons of online brokers' dealing costs and services, go to the Web site of Money extra (www.moneyextra.com) and click on online trading.

A broker's charging structure may vary depending on the size of deals. If the firm has no minimum charge, it will probably charge less for small deals but more for larger ones. If you are an occasional, small investor, use such a broker. Conversely, if the broker has a substantial minimum charge, it will typically charge less if you trade in large sizes.

Costs should not be your only selection criteria. For instance, some cheaper brokers deal only at specified times in the day to cut costs. You may find this acceptable if you make occasional small trades, but not if you are investing more seriously.

Some firms charge for other services, including money transfers, having an account and processing share certificates.

Limit orders

Use a broker that accepts limit orders. These are when you ask your broker to buy shares at or less than a specified price, or to sell at or above a specified price. If this is impossible, your broker will cancel the order. Brokers such as James Brearley and FasTrade accept limit orders that they keep open for the day. Brokers such as Xest accept limit orders on a fill-or-kill basis, which means they either execute the order immediately at the price specified, or cancel it.

The alternative to a limit order is a market order. This is *at best*, which means at the best price available for you. But prices change rapidly. Given the potential delay before your order is processed, and the impact of other orders ahead of you in the queue, you may end up paying more than the claimed real-time price quoted on a browser-based broker's screen.

Trading hours

All brokers deal during London market trading hours (8.00 am to 4.30 pm, Monday–Friday). Some also deal outside these hours. If so, they will process the order first thing the following morning, which is at a time when prices of FTSE-100 stocks can fluctuate wildly (see later in this module). For this reason, if you trade out of hours, use a limit order.

Fantasy trading

Some brokers offer facilities for fantasy or paper trading, which involves going through the motions of trading but without committing real money. This simulated exercise can be a useful experience, but it is not the same as the real thing.

Also useful is a good demo, which takes you through how to place an order. There are excellent demos at the Web sites of online brokers Selftrade (www.selftrade.com) and DLJ Direct (www.dljdirect.co.uk).

New equity issues

Sometimes, your online broker will give you access to new equity issues. This can be a double-edged sword as many new issues are suspect regarding timing and pricing, and institutions are usually given priority allocation. Before you invest in new issues, make sure you have completed Day 7, where we review the subject in depth.

Provision of financial news, data and similar

Some online brokers have all-singing-and-all-dancing Web sites giving lots of research, news flow, and investment education. Do not judge the broker too much on its level of such peripheral services. You can usually obtain similar material free elsewhere on the Web.

One-stop financial shopping

Online brokers are already becoming more like banks. They will give you a good rate of interest on your cash balance and, in some cases, a cheque book. Check these facilities if they are important to you.

US dealing facilities

If you want to deal in US stocks, check that your broker will do this, and at what price. Alternatively, open an account with a US broker. One of the cheapest is Ameritrade which, at the time of writing, has a flat fee of US $8 for online traders, including those from overseas. In the United States, the bid–offer spread quoted on stocks is typically lower than in the UK.

You will also need to fill in a W-8 form which exempts you from paying US taxes. As an investor in US shares, you will be taking a risk on the sterling/dollar exchange rate, as well as on the performance of the shares. This can work for you as well as against you. You will pay no stamp duty on purchases.

US brokers usually offer margin trading. This enables you to put up only a small part of the amount that you will invest in a stock, so magnifying your percentage gains or losses. Some UK brokers now offer the same facility.

For more about dealing in US stocks, consult the Web site of Nasdaq (www.nasdaq.co.uk). This is the high-tech market that sets the pace for all of the so-called new markets specializing in high-tech stocks across Europe, including TechMARK in the UK, the Nouveau Marche in France, the NeuerMarkt in Germany and the Nuovo Mercato in Italy. At the time of writing, Nasdaq has negotiated the acquisition of a majority stake in Easdaq, the Belgium-based pan-European exchange.

The United States leads and the rest of the world follows. For commentary on the US markets, many of the best Web sites available across the world are at your disposal. I suggest you start with the user-friendly Motley Fool US Web site (www.fool.com). Use this site for news, share prices, investor education and analysis. But do not make any one financial Web site your only source of information. Ultimately, you must take responsibility for your own investment decisions.

For specific, up-to-date comparisons

The information required to compare individual brokers rapidly becomes dated, but it is all accessible online so you can make your own comparisons at any given time.

The leading online brokers advertise their services widely over the Net. For a direct comparison of brokers and their services, go to the Gomez Web site (www.gomez.com, and click into the UK section). Also go to the UK Motley Fool Web site (www.fool.co.uk) which has a useful table comparing costs of online brokers. On its message boards, you will find a great deal of informal feedback.

The mechanics of dealing

Get online

If you are not online, you will need an Internet service provider (ISP) to enable this. You can get a free CD from shops which, once installed, will give you the necessary Internet access. The most usual deal – suitable for all but the frequent users – is that you will pay no subscription, but call charges. For frequent users, ISPs usually provide an option of paying a monthly subscription and having your calls otherwise free.

Update your computer

If your computer is old, or your Web browser is out of date, do the necessary upgrades. You cannot afford inferior technology when buying and selling shares. The speed at which you conduct a trade may be crucial.

Open your online account

To open your online account, you will need the relevant form. As we saw on Day 1, you can download this from your chosen broker's Web site. Otherwise, e-mail the firm, asking it to send you the form by e-mail.

Once you have printed off the form, fill it in and sign it by hand, as the firm usually prefers a handwritten signature. Send your completed form to the broker. You should enclose money – typically a minimum of £1,000 – to open your account and provide initial dealing funds. You can transfer further funds to and from your designated bank account only.

The firm will issue you as a new client with a welcome pack and password. It will hold your money in an interest-paying account pending your first trade.

Obtain a dealing price

To obtain a price on a stock, you will have to type in the name of the company or, more usually, its EPIC code, in the box provided. The EPIC code is an abbreviated three or four letter symbol which you can look up quickly on your broker's Web site.

You should then be able to access a spread for the company in question on the screen of your online broker. Your broker will have obtained this spread from the market makers. Sometimes when you ask for a price, the broker will quote the spread, but when you go through the process of dealing, will quote just the bid or offer price.

You will be able to deal in shares quoted on the London Stock Exchange in at least the normal market size (NMS), which is the minimum number of shares for which a market maker must quote firm bid and offer prices. As a general rule, the smaller the stock, the smaller the NMS, and the wider the spread. This correlation is because the market maker finds smaller stocks less easy to buy and sell.

Brokers may be linked to only one market maker and may not get you the best price. Unlike other brokers, Barclays scans the main market makers in a stock to obtain the best price.

You will be able to deal in the largest UK companies, which make up the entire FTSE-100 index, at relatively narrow spreads. This is because brokers use the SETS order book for these stocks instead of dealing with market makers. Avoid dealing in FTSE-100 stocks early in the morning or late in the afternoon, when their prices can become volatile due to temporary imbalance (see earlier in this module).

Get your order right

It is generally a good idea to place a limit order. This way, you will not risk dealing at a price beyond your control, as with a market order. But do not set the limit too low on a stock that you really want to buy, or you may end up with nothing.

When you place your order, get it right. If you order 30,000 shares when you had intended 3,000, this may not be retrievable. If you make such an error, get in touch with your broker immediately – to save time, by telephone. At worst, the broker will probably do a cancelling trade, and you will have to pay the difference from price movement as well as two sets of commission.

Some brokers offer a facility for retracting your order for a few seconds after you have placed it. This can give you peace of mind, but it is irksome for frequent traders as it slows down the order placement. Also, some brokers run an online facility to ensure that you don't spend more on shares than you can afford, or sell shares that you do not own, and similar.

Settlement

Once you have dealt, you will need to settle within a specified period, which in February 2000 was shortened from five to three days. This is known as T+3 settlement. If you have share certificates, which in the UK account for only 15 per cent of all transactions, the settlement period remains ten days (T+10).

In all cases, settlement is electronic, through the Crest computerized system, which matches trades with payments and informs the underlying company's registrar of changes to the share register. The system has occasionally gone wrong.

Once you have dealt, you will be able to print your contract note off the screen. Keep this as a hard copy. It contains details of the trade and commission charged, as well as stamp duty (charged at 0.5 per cent of purchase value when you buy UK shares, but inapplicable when you sell them).

Share certificates or nominee accounts

Online brokers prefer to hold your shares electronically through a pooled nominee account, and some insist on this. Taking this route, you will have your shares registered in the name of a nominee company run by your broker, but you will retain beneficial ownership of the shares.

However, as a nominee shareholder you will forfeit the right to receive full shareholder perks, including an annual report and accounts, and the right to vote at shareholder meetings. It is your broker's name that will be placed on your holding, and the company is not even aware that you hold the shares. You will still receive dividends and regular account statements.

As an alternative, enabling you to receive full shareholder perks, you may have a Crest-sponsored member account. In this case, you will be electronically registered as a Crest member and will incur an annual charge directly from the London Stock Exchange, rather than from your broker. When you trade shares, it will be your details, and not your broker's, that are passed electronically with the transaction. However, your broker maintains this account on your behalf.

Some investors find it most satisfying to hold paper certificates. If you are among them, you will need to find a broker that is happy with dealing on this basis, and ideally does not charge highly for it. On completing a deal, you will have to send the certificates through the post, which brings a slight risk of loss. The settlement process is slower than when using a nominee account.

Once you are a shareholder

Dividends

Most larger companies quoted on the markets pay a dividend. This represents a pay out from profits to shareholders. It takes place twice a year in the UK. The share price rises a little as the so-called Dividend Day approaches, and falls after the dividends have been distributed. The shares then become ex-dividend.

If you are due a dividend on shares held with your online broker, the money should be put straight into your account. You can check online that this has been done. The broker should send you a consolidated dividend tax certificate at the end of the financial year.

Rights issues

A rights issue is relevant for you only when you already hold shares in a company. It takes place when a company wants to raise funds from existing shareholders. You will have the right to buy new shares at slightly less than the current value of your existing shares, and without paying a broker's commission.

If, for example, you are offered a 1 for 2 rights issue, this gives you the right to buy one new share for every two that you already hold. Alternatively, you can sell your rights in the market, or let them lapse and later receive a cheque from the company for the amount involved. Afterwards, the share price of the underlying company will even out at slightly below that of your original shares.

Your online broker will inform you of any rights issue for which you are eligible, and you can confirm any participation by e-mail. First, however, ask why the company wants the funding. If it is for unwise expansion or another wrong reason, steer clear. Should directors not take up a rights issue, it is often wise to follow their example.

Scrip issues

Your broker will inform you of any scrip issue affecting your holding. A scrip issue – also known as bonus or capitalization issue

– is designed to increase the marketability and therefore liquidity of a company's shares by reducing the share price without compromising aggregate value. It takes the form of an issue of free shares, and there is an accompanying technical change to the company's balance sheet.

After a scrip issue, you will find, upon logging in, that you have more shares but at a proportionately lower share price. The overall value of your holding – unlike after a rights issue – will be the same. At least that is the theory.

In practice the overall value of your shares may become a little higher because there is a psychological value attached to scrip issues. Investors illogically believe that more shares at an adjusted lower price – as you will receive, following a scrip issue – are more valuable than higher priced shares of the same total value.

Takeovers

Your broker should let you know by e-mail of takeover action affecting a company in which you hold shares. Companies that are actual or rumoured takeover targets often see their share price soar over a short space of time. This could be within minutes or hours, or it could be within days. You can make quick money if you buy early, and sell out after the share price has risen nicely but before the speculation has subsided. This is a risky investment practice in which timing is crucial and luck plays a part. If a takeover rumour is quashed, the share price can drop like a stone.

In the late 1990s, colleagues of mine on the trading floor of a leading investment bank had a field day as they cashed in on cross-border takeover talks across Europe between financial services groups and telecoms companies. These exciting days are gone, but will be back sooner than some people think.

Get streetwise about tax

Once you have bought your shares online, you can put them in an ISA. This is a government-backed tax-efficient wrapper for your shares and/or other investments. All ISAs must be held in nominee accounts.

Any shares held in an ISA are entirely protected from capital gains tax. Until 2004 only, the ISA manager will be able to claim a 10 per cent income tax credit on dividends from shares on your behalf.

You can invest your entire ISA allowance (£7,000 per year) in shares, and change these indefinitely within the ISA, subject to related charges. Try to buy shares for your ISA directly. If you already own shares and want to put them in an ISA, you are letting yourself in for an expensive hassle. You will have to sell the shares, incurring CGT liability, then put the cash into your ISA, and buy them back, complete with dealing costs.

Make sure too that you net your losses – including those brought forward from previous years – against capital gains. Separately, you can transfer shares to your marriage partner tax-free.

For further information on ISAs, visit the very useful Web site of the Inland Revenue (www.inlandrevenue.gov.uk), where you will also find other advice on tax planning. Go also to www.isa-selector.co.uk, part of Moneyscene.co.uk, which has a very clear presentation on how ISAs work.

Complaints

These days, UK-based stockbrokers are authorized by the Securities and Futures Authority (SFA). A few share dealing firms are authorized by the Personal Investment Authority (PIA).

If a firm has shown incompetence or dishonesty in its dealings with you, you have grounds for complaint. Every stockbroker is obliged to have a written complaints procedure in place. Sometimes this does not work well. If so, you realistically have two options.

Your first complaint option is to approach the regulators. The complaints procedure against UK stockbrokers is outlined on the SFA's Web site (www.sfa.org.uk). Essentially, an industry complaints bureau can mediate between the firm and yourself, and attempt to come to a resolution. If this fails, the next step would be arbitration, which is strictly at the option of yourself as client, or court action – not usually both.

I once used the SFA's mediation service against a broker and found it effective. However, I refused the first two offers that the mediator obtained from the firm, and sent him back to negotiate a better deal. Eventually, I received a satisfactory offer. Never accept the mediator's word as final.

At the time of writing, the SFA and the PIA are about to merge with others into the Financial Services Authority (FSA), which will serve as the sole regulatory authority for the entire UK financial services authority. By the time you are reading this, the new structure will probably be in place. Check out the FSA's Web site at www.fsa.gov.uk. Its helpline is 0845 606 1234.

Your second complaint option is to take the matter to the press or TV. For obvious reasons, even a threat of this can bring a swift result. If you need to proceed, I advise you to go to national newspapers or TV, where exposure will hit the firm hardest. You would do well to choose Sunday papers where the journalists have extra time to research their stories.

In all cases, you will complain more effectively if you have a record of deals and conversations with your broker. Keep careful notes. Marshall your facts, so that you can present them coherently.

The industry compensation scheme

If your SFA-registered stockbroker defaults, you will have access to the industry's compensation scheme. The first £30,000 of any proven claim will be met in full, and 90 per cent of the next £20,000 will be met – with £48,000 being the maximum compensation paid to any single claimant. Overall, the fund will not pay out more than £100 million in any single year.

The way forward

As an online stock market investor, you are in control. Do not lose this. Do not place your trades outside hours except through a limit order. Keep your password secret. Know all the charges that you are incurring. Make sure that your broker has strong security. Make full use of your account's facilities and do not necessarily be loyal to your broker. This way, you will run your account. It will not run you.

Dynamic rules of the Online Share Buyer's FlexiSystem

- Online brokers are cheap, permanently accessible, fast, and will deal in small sizes. But they usually require you to make your own investment decisions, and this can be risky.
- The mobile Internet gives you stock market news and dealing facilities on-the-move but is at this stage limited.
- To compare online brokers, go to the Gomez Web site (www.gomez.com). Do not select your broker on cost grounds only.
- Avoid online brokers that are glorified e-mail services. Go for active trader brokers if you deal frequently, or otherwise browser-based operations.
- Use a broker that has a telephone back-up service, and open an account with another broker as a further back-up.
- Make sure that your broker uses 128-bit encryption software, which will give your transactions maximum security. Your broker should also have insurance in place.
- Make the password that you use with your broker a nonsense word. Keep it secret.
- For efficient share dealing, make sure that your computer equipment is reasonably up to date.
- When you have completed a transaction, print out the contract note for your records.
- It is generally a good idea to place a limit order, particularly if you deal out of hours.
- Do not judge your broker too much on the amount of free material on its Web site.
- For commentary on the US markets, start with using the Motley Fool US Web site (www.fool.com).
- Transactions involving paper share certificates are now time-consuming and sometimes expensive.
- It is more efficient to hold your shares electronically in a pooled nominee account, although this means you will forfeit the right to full shareholder perks.
- Query the reason for a rights issue on shares you hold and, if it is not satisfactory, steer clear.
- Only deal with *bona fide* stock brokers which, at the time of writing, are authorized by the SFA.

- You can make quick money on takeover rumours. But you need to buy and sell the affected shares at the right time.
- Consider putting your shares in an ISA for tax efficiency if you are planning on holding them for the long term.

Day 3

Become your own online equities analyst

Overview

Before you buy shares, you should have some understanding what they are worth. Without this knowledge, you might be paying far too much. To avoid this trap, you should become your own equities analyst. In this spirit, I will today show you how to apply basic analytical techniques to a company in which you are considering investing.

First, we will take an overview of a company's annual report and accounts. It is essential that you are able to get to grips with this at least in outline as it is the basis for understanding a company's financial situation. Next, we will look at the key ratios that you will be using to value companies, taking the figures from the accounts. These will enable you to assess how profitable the company is, how much ready cash it has, and how its managers have performed.

We will run through the basics of discounted cash-flow analysis, which is the favoured professional way to value companies. We will look at special rules that apply to Internet company valuation, and the broader, macro-economic perspective. Finally we will look at how to obtain analysts' reports, including through online resources, and how to screen stocks.

To pave the way for all this, let us assess the difference between value investing and growth investing, and why they both require fundamental analysis.

Value and growth investing

Overlap between value and growth investing

Online investment gurus often categorize value investing and growth investing separately. In reality, the overlap is significant. If a stock is a bargain on fundamental grounds, it should also have some growth prospects. Conversely, a good growth stock should ideally have fundamental value.

Despite this, the value investor has different priorities from the growth investor. As a value investor, you will select stocks by applying ratio analysis. If a stock is cheap on fundamentals compared to its peers, you will buy the shares and wait until the share price rises to reflect true value.

In practice, this usually happens, but it might take a long time. Value investing requires patience. Furthermore, you are taking risks, as shares are usually depressed for a reason. Two apparently outstanding value investments, Iceland and Independent Insurance, issued profit warnings in early 2001, and in both cases the share price plummeted. This came as a severe shock to those who had patted themselves on the back for buying bargain shares.

To minimize this kind of risk, never just buy a stock because it is fundamentally cheap. Also look for some growth prospects, and evidence that the company is not experiencing serious business problems. In this way, our kind of value investing involves qualitative as well as quantitative assessments.

Growth investing has a reputation for being both riskier and more exciting than value investing. As a growth investor, you will buy stocks which are rising sharply in value, or have the potential to do so. On fundamentals, the shares may be overvalued. The logic is that the market has priced the shares high for a reason, and so long as that reason holds valid, they will continue to outperform.

Whether you are a value or a growth investor, you will need to use ratio analysis to find suitable stocks. Some services will calculate ratios on your behalf. I particularly recommend *REFS*, which stands for Really Essential Financial Statistics. This reference book, published by Hemmington Scott, is revised monthly. The online version is at www.hemscott.co.uk.

You can also find stocks that satisfy your ratio criteria using a stock screening device online. But to understand what the ratios mean, you must learn to calculate them yourself. This module will cover the basics.

The framework of the annual report and accounts

The figures included in ratios are in most cases taken from the company report and accounts, which most UK-quoted companies issue twice a year. After the first six months, whose starting date will vary, an interim statement will be published. Soon after the full year, the company publishes full year figures, known as preliminaries, followed by the official audited annual report and accounts.

The first major item in the annual report is the chairman's statement, which is typically full of hype about the company. However, it may contain veiled warnings. Learn to read between the lines. At the end, you will find the auditor's report. This normally tells you that everything is true and fair, although in some cases it may not be strictly accurate. If something is seriously wrong, the auditor qualifies the accounts. This should always make you wary.

Within this framework, the most important part of the accounts are its three main financial statements: the profit and loss account, the balance sheet and the cash flow statement. You should read these in conjunction with the numbered notes at the back of the report and accounts. Here you will find the things the company is required to tell you but prefers not to include in the glossy part at the front.

In each of the three main financial statements, the current year's figures are shown alongside the previous year's for comparison purposes. We will look at each statement in turn.

The profit and loss account

The profit and loss account records the company's profits or losses, and how they were reached, over the previous year. It starts with turnover, which is all income received by the company. Cost of sales and other expenses are deducted on a net basis from turnover to give the trading profit. After deduction of interest, we have pre-tax profit.

After tax and dividends, this becomes net profit. The net profit figure is used in the earnings per share ratio, which we will cover later in this module. The net profit margin, which is net profit divided by sales, will ideally be rising steadily every year. Most companies pay out some of their net profit in dividends and reinvest the rest. We will look at dividends again later.

The balance sheet

The balance sheet presents a financial snapshot of the company on only one day of its year. This may not be typical for the year as a whole. Here you will find the company's assets less liabilities on the top half of the balance sheet, balanced by shareholders' funds on the bottom half. The assets on the balance sheet include fixed and current assets.

Fixed assets may be tangible, such as land and machinery. Alternatively they may be intangible, such as brands (for which it is hard to find agreement on valuation) or goodwill, which is the difference between the purchase price of an acquired company and its net asset value. Current assets include stock, debtors and cash in hand. Stock has unreliable valuations, and debtors can be awkward about paying, which leaves cash as the most useful current asset.

After assets, come liabilities, which show what the company owes. Current liabilities, which are payable within one year, include trade creditors and overdrafts. We will next find the total of all assets less current liabilities. From this figure are deducted long-term liabilities, which are loans that do not need to be paid within a year.

The company's total assets less total liabilities on the balance sheet amount to its net assets. The net assets are balanced by various kinds of capital and reserves – described as shareholders' funds – in the bottom half of the balance sheet. The figures must balance, with net assets invariably equal to shareholders' funds.

The cash-flow statement

The cash-flow statement shows how much hard cash is available to the company. A company's net operating cash flow cannot be manipulated by creative accounting and may therefore be much less than the trading profit.

We will now look at some of the most important ratios for evaluating a company, and there is no better place to start than the earnings per share.

Pulling power of a steadily rising earnings per share

The earnings per share (eps) is the company's after-tax profits – culled from the profit and loss account – divided by the number of shares in issue. Analysts recalculate this figure regularly based on forecast after-tax profits, as well as on the latest confirmed figures. Broadly speaking, the City looks for an eps that rises steadily, even if slowly, year by year, and rewards companies that achieve this.

Does that mean that companies with a rising eps are good investments? In the short term, probably yes. In the long term, it depends. The problem is that accountants sometimes use legal but frowned-on techniques to restructure the accounts in order to create a steadily rising eps. This practice falls into the category of creative accounting.

Creative accounting – whitewashing poor financials

To increase earnings per share, accountants need to increase earnings and/or to reduce the shares in issue (which benefit from earnings). One way to enhance earnings is to increase the period over which a company's assets are depreciated (reduced in value to account for wear and tear). On a year-by-year basis, this will reduce the percentage depreciation that hits the profit and loss account.

Alternatively, tax payable in a given year can often be changed. Expenses can be smoothed. These techniques represent only a small proportion of those available for legally manipulating the accounts, although the Accounting Standards Board has over the last 10 years stamped out some of the more obvious such practices.

Sometimes, the City notices creative accounting in a favoured company only after the directors have issued a profits warning. In such cases, the market will typically overreact and the share price may fall by perhaps 50 per cent instantly. The analysts will be forced to revise their profit forecasts for the company. This will make most more cautious about recommending its shares in the future.

For a little more about creative accounting, of which manipulating the earnings per share is only a small part, please turn to Day 6, where it is discussed in the context of small companies. In terms of general ratio analysis, the eps is important not just in its own right but also because it forms part of the most widely used criterion of all, the price/earnings (PE) ratio.

The PE ratio

The PE ratio is made up of the underlying company's current share price, divided by its earnings per share. The eps figure used can be historic (past) or prospective (estimated for the future). The PE ratio shows how the market rates a company. If the company's PE ratio is low compared with that of its peers, the shares are looking cheap. They could be good value, but are very likely depressed for a reason.

Conversely, if the company's PE ratio is high compared with that of its peers, the shares are looking expensive. However, the market may have rated the shares so highly for a good reason. Whichever way, the shares will typically shoot higher in the short term but drop back ultimately.

How do you measure a PE ratio against that of its peers? The simplest way is to see how much higher or lower it is than the sector or market average. A reference source such as *REFS* does the job for you. This directory lists a given company's prospective PE – based on the next 12 months' consensus forecast eps – comparing it to the sector and to the market as a whole. The prospective PE is more up to date than the historic figure as it takes the future analysts' earnings forecasts into account. But it is also less reliable as these forecasts can be wrong.

The historic PE is listed in the newspapers and, to find the sector and market averages for comparison purposes, you should look at the FT's Actuaries Share Indices (The UK Series) in Monday's *Financial Times*.

Some professional analysts make more use of the PE ratio than others in their assessment of stocks. But none rely on it completely. A favourite criticism of the PE ratio is that it does not take account of growth. To address this deficiency, some favour the memorably named PEG ratio.

A PEG to hang your valuation on

The PEG is the contribution to investment analysis made by popular (and wealthy) UK investment guru Jim Slater. It shows a company's prospective PE ratio in relation to the growth rate of its earnings per share. This could be prospective growth, or historic. The PEG is best applied to small growth companies. If it is significantly less than one, this may represent value.

Net assets can matter

When you are evaluating property companies, investment trusts, or composite insurers, avoid relying on earnings-related ratios such as the eps, PE or PEG. Instead, use the share price/net asset value (NAV) per share as a measure of value. This is measured as the total assets of the company less its liabilities, debentures and loan stocks (taken from the balance sheet), divided by the number of shares in issue. If a company is trading on a low share price/NAV, it may be a bargain, but this may also be for a reason. You must probe.

In addition, check how the net asset figure is made up as it is not always updated. For example, properties may be historically valued on the balance sheet, but worth more as a result of capital gains. Machinery may be valued too low due to a conservative depreciation policy which knocks too much off its value.

When you invest on the stock market, you will probably look not just for capital gain, but also for income. You will receive this in dividends.

The dividend

Many quoted companies pay shareholders a dividend, which is a pay-out from profits to shareholders. In the UK this comes twice a year, in the United States, quarterly. The share price rises a little as the so-called Dividend Day approaches, and then falls after the dividend has been distributed and the shares technically become ex-dividend.

Some companies decline to pay a dividend. Small companies, in particular, may be growing so fast that they prefer to reinvest all their earnings in their own projects. If this results in a soaring share price, it can make far more for you in capital gain than you would ever make in income from dividends. The grandfather of all growth companies, Microsoft, has to date not paid a dividend.

If a stock does pay a dividend, you should assess this against the sector or the market as a whole. For this you need the company's gross yield, which is the gross annual dividend expressed as a percentage of the share price.

Institutional investors like to see a dividend that rises steadily every year, just as they want for the eps. A quoted company that is in the habit of paying dividends must pay lip service. If it does not regularly increase its dividend, or cuts it, this is a danger sign.

A liquidity check

A company may cut its dividend if its liquidity – availability of usable cash – is low. How do you measure a company's liquidity? The easiest check is the current ratio, defined as current assets divided by current liabilities (figures available on the balance sheet). As a rule of thumb, this should be at least two. In addition, the quick ratio (acid test), which is current assets less stock and work-in-progress divided by current liabilities, should ideally be over one.

Another sign of a pending dividend cut is when the dividend is not covered by the company's earnings. This means that the company must dip into reserves to pay it. To play safe, the dividend cover, which is earnings per share divided by dividend per share, should be at least one.

If the market knows of or suspects a pending dividend cut, it will mark down the share price. Once a company's share price falls, its gross yield rises. Low price blue chips with high yields are a popular contrarian investment. They are out-of-favour and the share price has fallen accordingly. The flip side is that the dividend has risen, which will benefit investors. Michael O'Higgins, a fund manager based in Albany, New York, popularized a technique for investing in such stocks in his book *Beating the Dow*, (HarperCollins).

UK investment guru Jim Slater has introduced the so-called O'Higgins method to UK investors in recent years. Taken over a long period, various versions of this investment system have beaten the major indices, which most fund managers fail to do. More recently the O'Higgins method has not worked so well in the UK, perhaps partly because it became too widely followed.

You will often find quoted companies in the high-tech and telecommunications industries that have neither yield nor earnings. Mobile telephone operators, for instance, are typically paying interest on high levels of debt. This is quite normal due to the capital-intensive nature of the business.

Analysts value such companies using enterprise value (market capitalization plus debt less cash) or EV, divided by earnings before interest, tax, depreciation and amortization (EBITDA). This ratio appropriately ignores interest payments for these companies' huge borrowings. It is essentially a cash-flow-related measure, which is useful, although not formally recognized by accountants.

In all companies, analysts assess management performance. One ratio which covers this is the return on capital employed (ROCE).

Performance of the company's managers

The return on capital employed is calculated as profits before interest payable and tax, divided by capital employed. The profits figure, which excludes elements outside management control, is taken from the profit and loss account. The capital employed is year-end total assets less total liabilities excluding long-term loans. The figures are taken from the balance sheet.

The higher a company's ROCE, the better the company is using the assets at its disposal. Ideally, the figure should be rising year-on-year, and should compare favourably with that of the company's peers.

Evidence of over-borrowing

You should also investigate a company's level of borrowing, known as gearing. You can do this with the gearing ratio. This is defined as interest bearing loans and preference share capital, divided by ordinary shareholders' funds, all expressed as a percentage. Become concerned if gearing is significantly over 50 per cent without a good reason.

Cash is king

In the accounting context, it is a truism that profits are opinion, and cash is fact. You cannot disguise how much hard cash a company has. If it does not have enough, it will go under, regardless of its potential, its revenues, or even its profits. A number of Internet companies have found this out the hard way.

You should therefore look for cash flow in a company. This is so even if its market valuation derives from its business model, its market share, or something else far removed. Let me give you an example.

In November 1999, I recommended that readers of *Vanguard Investor*, a high-tech tip sheet for which I was writing, should buy shares in Geo Interactive Media, an Israeli broadband company quoted on the London Stock Exchange at around 300p.

The appeal of Geo Interactive was in its business model, and that it was a leader in the high-demand field of streaming technology, which speeds up the transfer of so-called rich media – video and sound transmission – via the Internet. But I made a point of also checking the company's cash flow.

Geo Interactive was spending US $1.2 million a month from a basis of US $21 million net cash. At that rate, its cash burn (rate of cash expenditure) would last until the end of 2000. However, plenty of cash-enhancing deals lay ahead, and the company's own prediction that it would soon be cash-positive seemed plausible.

Sure enough, in October 2000, the company reported that it had net cash of US $381 million, partly as a result of an acquisition strategy in the first half of that year –taking full control of Orca Interactive and Zapex Research – that enhanced cash flow. In the year since I had recommended the stock it had risen in value from 300p to 1400p.

When I originally recommended Geo Interactive, I made an inspired (and informed) guess that the company would increase its cash flow. It was not possible to do more. For more mature companies, you can look at present levels of cash flow.

A useful ratio for this purpose is cash flow per share, divided by earnings per share. You can obtain these figures from the company's financial statements, or *REFS* calculates the ratio for you. If the result is more than one, you will have pinpointed likely value in the underlying company.

Professional analysts prefer to use a more scientific method for forecasting cash flow. This is discounted cash flow (DCF) analysis, which translates prospective cash flows into present value. By so including the time value of money, it has the edge over simpler cash-flow measuring techniques.

If you are to conduct your own DCF analysis, you must first find the company's net operating cash flow (NOCF). This involves taking earnings before interest and tax (EBIT). Deduct from this corporation tax paid and capital expenditure. Add depreciation and amortization, which do not represent a movement of cash outside the company. Then add or subtract the overall change in working capital, including movements in stock, in debtors and creditors, and in cash or cash equivalents.

The result is the NOCF for this year. You should also calculate this for future years. Obviously, due to inflation, cash available next year is worth less in present day terms than if it was available this year. In addition, cash flow will continue into the future, beyond the perhaps five or ten years over which the DCFs are spread.

The cash flows covering the period beyond are known as the terminal value and, without evidence to the contrary, are assumed to extend into infinity. Present and future cash flows and terminal value combined make up a company's present value.

The DCF method is not perfect. In discounting future cash flows, you will not necessarily come up with an accurate net present value. The accuracy will depend partly on how reliable are the forecasts used for NOCF, with the reliability being nil for young, high-tech companies. It will also depend on how many years are included in the DCF analysis. Another factor is the rate at which you discount the cash flows. The larger this rate is, the smaller is the net present value of future cash flows. This discount rate – also known as required rate of return – can be compared with the same figure for other investment proposals.

How do you select an appropriate discount rate? One way is to use the same rate as comparable companies use. However, this method has proved unreliable because it is hard to make accurate comparisons. A more reliable method – widely used by professional investors – is to use the company's weighted average cost of capital (WACC) as the discount rate.

So what is the WACC? Generally, companies raise their capital through equity or debt. The WACC represents the cost of capital to the company weighted in terms of debt and equity. We can break down the WACC into its two components. First, the cost of debt is the current yield to maturity on the company's bonds. Second, the cost of equity is commonly measured by the Capital Asset Pricing Model (CAPM – pronounced CAPEM).

The CAPM is widely used but controversial. It assumes that investors should be rewarded for acquiring investments which carry a larger amount of *market* risk, which cannot be diversified away. The higher a share's market risk, the higher is its so-called beta. If a share fluctuates in line with the market, it will have a beta of 1. If it has a beta of 2.0 or 0.5, it will fluctuate proportionately more or less than the market.

Unfortunately, beta is an historical figure and so not always reliable. Therefore, a portfolio of high beta stocks does not always outperform one of low beta stocks as it should. In practice, beta works better over a period (decades rather than years) or at times of major share price fluctuation such as during a market crash.

With the unreliability of the CAPM contributing to uncertainty about what is the right discount rate, many analysts plot a range of DCF models using several discount rates. This way, they can present some alternatives. Even then, some analysts abuse DCF analysis to paint an over-optimistic picture of a favoured company's prospects.

At the beam-end of the market, there are false DCF projections for companies that have no hope of generating cash flow or even plans to do so. Crooks are trying to push shares in these companies onto unsuspecting private investors via the Internet.

Qualitative factors

While some value investors focus purely on ratio and DCF analysis, others mix this with a strong dose of qualitative assessment. I would strongly recommend that you also look beyond just the figures. A stock is sometimes cheap for a good reason, as investors in Marks & Spencer have found in recent years to their cost, buying shares only to see them plummet in value.

Invest in a present market leader. If you do so, you will often pay more. But, provided that the company is capable of maintaining its leadership, you are likely to make more money in the long run.

Also, look for management with a strong track record, and be wary of any past links with failure or fraud. In hard times particularly, experience counts. Check out the age of key managers and their backgrounds. If, for example, the chief executive is in his late forties, he is young enough to stay with the company for the foreseeable future, but mature enough to have experience and judgement.

Internet companies

Many Internet companies have no profits, and some have almost no revenues. They are young and unpredictable. For these and other reasons, analysts apply special rules when valuing such companies. These include, for instance, how many visitors the company's Web site attracts. There are various methods of measuring this, each of which produces a different figure.

One of the more credible measures of valuation is the price/sales ratio (PSR). This is the total market capitalization of the company (share price × number of shares in issue) divided by last year's sales (as on the profit and loss account in the most recent annual report and accounts). This ratio could be 5 or 6, or less. It could be as high as 30 or 40, or more. The only way to assess whether the PSR is too high or low is by comparing it with that of the company's peers.

This ratio, although suitable for a sector that is not expected to be profitable in the early stages, has its limitations. Ultimately, sales are useless without profits. But if sales increase, so could market share, which should lead to profitability, the theory goes. In the next few years, we shall be finding out how far it is true of recently established Internet companies.

Because Internet and other young high-tech companies have such unpredictable future revenues, DCF analysis is often an unreliable way to value them. Many analysts prefer to look at comparables. In 1999 and early 2000, some saw real options pricing as a way to assess Internet companies.

Real option pricing

Real option pricing places a value on a company's flexibility to take appropriate actions in response to different scenarios. For example, a manufacturer can choose its market, and how to adapt its product to the market's needs. The various alternative routes to creating value – or real options – may be evaluated in advance.

To value real options, you need to capture the dynamics of uncertainty over a period, according to PriceWaterhouse Coopers, the accountancy firm that specializes in this area of valuation. It offers a way to do this through so-called decision trees. Each path in a tree is given a value, calculated by a cash-flow model.

Since the March 2000 correction in high-tech stock valuations, real option pricing has become much less popular. The problem is that real options provided over-optimistic recommendations on shares. This is because unreliable information was fed into the models.

Your choice of Internet companies

If you want to invest in Internet companies, go for the right sub-sector. Avoid business-to-consumer companies, which sell products and services to the public. These are suffering as competition has driven consumer prices of many popular products promoted via the Internet down to unprofitable levels. To a lesser extent, business-to-business, earlier heralded as the great hope for Internet companies, has proved a disappointment.

In both these sub-sectors, revenue to fund expansion, not to mention eventual profits, has to come from somewhere, and for all too many of these companies advertising is the only source. But advertisers have not shown enough interest. Some sites take subscriptions from users, but this too has not proved easy.

At the time of writing, it is the infrastructure companies, which provide services to the Internet sector, that are the most promising. Within this sub-sector, look for a sound business model. If it is modelled on that of a proven company, that can be a good sign. If a company is backed by top-name venture capitalists, this is a good sign, but it is by no means a fail-safe.

Do not be swayed by the favourable media attention that a company attracts as this can swiftly be reversed. The Internet leisure services company, lastminute.com, was a victim. When the company was floated in March 2000, it was the media's darling. The National Portrait Gallery in London displayed a photograph of its two youthful founders – Martha Lane Fox reclining on a sofa with her legs resting on Brent Hoberman's lap.

This did not stop the share price of lastminute.com from falling hard in early secondary market trading. The media revised its opinion of the company instantly. As you will read on Day 7, the flotation proved little short of a disaster for those subscribers who had failed to sell their holdings quickly.

Look at the wider picture

The role of interest rates

Be alert to macro-economic events that will affect the stock market. If, for example, the Bank of England announces that it will be cutting interest rates, this will benefit the stock market. It will mean cheaper borrowings for quoted companies, and many people will buy shares rather than leave their money on deposit for a lower return. Also, gilts will decline in value, which makes shares look comparatively cheap. Conversely, if the Bank of England raises interest rates, this will adversely affect shares.

If an interest rate change comes as a surprise, the UK stock market will show a knee-jerk reaction. If the market had expected this move, it will have 'discounted' it, and so will not react so strongly. For its part, the Bank of England will often try to signal a rate change in advance. It will have made the decision on the basis of more than one inflationary indicator. Here are some of the key inflationary indicators:

- Gross Domestic Product (GDP). This measures national income and is revised quarterly. It is grossed because it does not allow for depreciation of capital. When the net value of income from abroad is included, the figure becomes Gross National Product (GNP). If GDP rises over 3 per cent in each of four quarters in succession, this sends a strong inflationary warning and the Bank of England will probably raise interest rates.

- Retail Price Index (RPI). Every month, the Office for National Statistics releases the RPI, which measures the price rises for a basket of goods, averaged on a weighted basis. This is a major inflation indicator. Besides the headline RPI, there is RPI-X, which is the headline figure excluding mortgage rates. There is also RPI-Y, which is RPI-X excluding indirect taxes such as VAT.
- The state of sterling. If sterling is strong, imported commodities, on which the UK relies heavily, are cheaper. This helps to keep inflation down.
- Average earnings index. The average earnings index is calculated quarterly on a seasonally adjusted basis, and is released on a two-month time lag. If it shows an annualized 4.5 per cent growth rate, this is consistent with the government's 2.5 per cent inflation target. A higher rate is a warning.
- Monthly unemployment count. Keep an eye on the monthly unemployment count. If unemployment is falling, this benefits quoted companies that rely on consumer spending. However, it is likely eventually to lead to a rise in interest rates to combat inflation.
- Money supply. Among economists, monetarists believe that controlling the money supply is the key to controlling inflation (as opposed to Keynsians who believe that it has little effect). UK money supply measures include M0, which represents narrow money – money in circulation plus sight deposits (current accounts with money available on demand). Another measure is M2, which is broad money (M0 plus savings deposits and time deposits).

Do I have to do all this work myself?

After this ratio and DCF analysis, not to mention the macro-economic perspective, I can hear you asking 'Is life as a serious investor worth living?' Well, contrary to what some financial Web sites claim, successful online investing is not easy. The good news is that once you have grasped the basic analytical tools covered in this module, you will find that you are automatically applying them. This is useful even if you never subsequently work out the ratios yourself, as you will be better able to assess the analysis of the professionals.

You cannot rely on the professionals

You should always be careful about relying on the judgement of the City and Wall Street professionals. With a few exceptions, they are not very good at stock selection. This is why equity-based unit trusts have a performance record that is, in at least 80 per cent of cases, below the market average, when management costs are deducted from the overall return.

Stockbroking analysts – more than their counterparts working for fund managers – must take a lion's share of the blame for selecting disappointing stocks. I know of one analyst specializing in an area of financial services who is the laughing stock of his firm, as he gets every one of his recommendations wrong. This does not stop him winning awards for the quality of his research.

In particular, do not rely on analysts' views on young Internet companies. In this sector, analysts have shown unjustified optimism, particularly in bull markets. They have, or hope to have, the companies in question as their corporate clients.

Across sectors, some analysts make better recommendations than others, just as some produce higher quality research, and these two are not always correlated. To find out which analysts are regarded as the leaders in their sector, and to examine their track record, visit the Institutional Investor Web site (www.iimagazine.com).

Once you understand its limitations, it is worth reading analysts' research for companies in which you are interested. You can obtain useful summaries of analysts' research reports in the magazine *Investors Chronicle*, although they will by this stage have already been digested (and acted on) by the professionals.

Analysts will sometimes discuss a specific company in their specialist sector with you directly, particularly if it is one that they follow closely. They may make available recent research reports, if you ask them directly. Telephone them – not before about 9.30 am, as they are at their busiest in the early morning. Ask the switchboard to transfer you to an analyst (ideally named) in a particular sector.

If you get through, ask brief and specific questions about your chosen company. Do not make them too basic or you will bore the analyst. What he or she says in response may be more frank and up to date than the most recent published research report. But ask to see the report as well. If possible, offer to collect it from his or her offices to save the analyst (or an over-worked assistant) the bother of posting it to you.

Alternatively, take the online route. For a broad span of analysts' research, which is again not always the latest, visit the relevant pay-as-you-go sites. The Thomson Financial Web site (www.thomson invest.net) offers access on this basis to research documents from banks and brokers (but not entirely from top firms). Multex Investor (www.multexinvestor.com) and FirstCall Research Direct (www.firstcall.com) provide similar services.

To find research on larger companies in particular, visit the Web sites of leading investment banks. Some of this material will be available free, but it may be a little out of date. Try the Web site of Merrill Lynch HSBC (www.mlhsbc.com). Unusually, Schroder Salomon Smith Barney (www.salomonsmithbarney.com) provides analysts' upgrades and downgrades online.

Among stockbrokers for small-to-medium-sized companies, Beeson Gregory (www.beeson-gregory.co.uk) offers online access to its research. Peel Hunt (www.peelhunt.com) has a research subscription service for private investors, including daily updates and video interviews with company executives. Outside stockbroking, a lively resource for the small company sector is itruffle (www.itruffle.com).

For recommendations in the high-tech sector, try Equity investigator (www.equityinvestigator.co.uk) where up to date, quality research is available on subscription. Durlacher (www.durlacher.com), the investment boutique, has offered free research online on the technology and media sectors, which varies in quality. Wit Soundview (www.witcapital.com or www.witsoundview.com), the online investment bank, offers free high-tech reports online. To keep up with high-tech developments, visit Redherring (www.redherring.com), the online version of the eponymous US high-tech industry magazine.

US research is available free from Merrill Lynch (www.ml.com) and Salomon Smith Barney (www.smithbarney.com). If you hold an account with stockbroker Charles Schwab (www.schwab.com) you can visit its Analyst centre, which makes its own research reports available, together with consensus earnings estimates. For free independent research, visit www.streetadvisor.com and www.

fertilemind.net. Also try Moneyguru (www.moneyguru.com) whose in-house analysts offer their own research reports.

Analysts consensus forecasts

In most cases, you must avoid investing in a company for which analysts have recently downgraded their earnings forecasts. Conversely, you should be encouraged by analysts' recent earnings upgrades.

To find analysts' consensus forecasts, consult REFS (www.hemscott.net), or Sharescope (www.sharescope.com). For related useful information about companies, visit www.investor-relations.co.uk.

Screening stocks

To screen stocks for required ratios and other criteria, I would recommend the stock screener at the Marketeye Web site which comes as part of a premium service at £10 a month. Marketeye's site is accessed through the Thomson Financial Network site (www.thomsonfn.com).

To use such a stock screener, you must first decide what levels you will set as limits. If, for example, you are looking for companies with a PE ratio of under 12 in a given sector, you can input this criterion, and find out which stocks fit the requirement.

If your requirements are more complicated, you can input your chosen combination of criteria, including perhaps current dividend yield, return on assets, net margin, current ratio, debt/equity ratio, and/or others.

If you want to screen US stocks, go to Quicken.com (www.quicken.com/investments/stocks). A more sophisticated US screening service is available at MarketGuide (www.marketguide.com). Alternatively, MarketPlayer.com (www.marketplayer.com/scrn) offers set filters based on the stock-picking methods of established gurus. These include the Warren Buffett Stable Growth screen, and the Ridiculously High Valuation screen.

The way forward

You have just completed *the most important module in the book*. To win as a medium- to long-term online investor, you must understand the companies in which you buy shares. For this you require a grasp of company accounting and ratio analysis.

I strongly recommend that you revisit this module sometimes and, once you are familiar with the principles covered, do some related further reading. On Day 12, I will give you some key book recommendations.

Dynamic rules of the Online Share Buyer's FlexiSystem

- There is some overlap between growth and value investing.
- The City rewards companies that achieve a steadily rising earnings per share. For this reason, some manipulate their earnings.
- In valuing property companies, investment trusts or composite insurers, take account of the net asset per share.
- Growth companies can often make more money for investors by reinvesting earnings instead of paying a dividend.
- If a company that regularly pays a dividend cuts it, this is a danger sign.
- A company needs a current ratio (current assets less current liabilities) of at least two as a sign of adequate liquidity.
- Become concerned if a company's gearing (borrowing) exceeds 50 per cent without a good reason.
- If a company has a rising return on capital employed, it is making efficient use of assets at its disposal.
- Make a priority in checking a company's cash flow, on the basis either of relevant ratios, or of DCF forecasts.
- Invest in companies that have strong, experienced management, some degree of market leadership, and growth potential as well as value.
- If you want to invest in Internet companies, go for the infrastructure sub-sector.
- A cut in interest rates benefits shares, and a rise has the opposite effect. The Bank of England will try to signal an intention to change interest rates.

- Be your own equities analyst – but keep an eye on the views of the professionals via the Internet or by calling the analyst directly.
- Use Internet resources to screen stocks.

Day 4
How to win as a share trader

Overview

Share trading is not for cissies. It is a high risk–high reward, fast-moving business that requires full attention, courage, and astute judgement, not to mention enough capital to cushion you against losses.

In this module we will look at day trading, swing trading, and position trading, and how they differ. We will look at, and learn from, the seven main mistakes that traders make. You will learn the practicalities of setting up as a trader, and of some useful Web sites. We will specify the most suitable type of online broker for your purposes.

You will discover how to place limit orders, and the basic rules of successful trading – including protection of your capital, and diversification. This module also covers when you should buy and when you should sell, and touches on self-development for traders, including in such areas as neuro-linguistic programming.

Gear up for sharing trading

A high risk business

As a share trader you can make – or lose – thousands of pounds in seconds. Your results will not always be so extreme, and sometimes may be more so. How far you succeed depends, paradoxically, more on you than on market conditions. But first, you must master the basics.

It is on the early learning curve that you are most likely to lose money. If you are a little scared, that is good, as it can make you be more careful. Otherwise, you must be independent, logical and decisive in sometimes volatile markets. In this way you will stand out from the herd of traders.

Your early trading efforts will also give you the opportunity to assess whether this game is right for you. As you become more involved in share trading, expect to risk losing not just your money but, with it, your friends, your status and perhaps your self-respect. If you have the stomach for share trading, you will enjoy the rocky ride. Stuart Watson, who has an outstanding record of trading equities through his US-based firm Reindeer Capital, believes that anyone can do the job of trading, and that you do not have to be born to do it. Many other top traders believe the same.

The most important part of your training is hard experience. It is through this, if at all, that you will develop the gut feeling on which so many top traders rely. But first you need to understand some principles. Applying these, you can avoid some expensive mistakes and take appropriate trading actions. Let us first survey the trading styles open to you.

Categories of share trading

Share trading breaks down into three broad categories: day, swing and position trading:

- As a day trader, you close out your position every day. This way, you will avoid the risk of holding shares overnight. You will thrive on market volatility.
- As a swing trader, you hold shares for between two and five days, which can give you more time for success, but also for failure.
- As a position trader, you will hold shares for between one and two months, which gives you still more flexibility.

Some traders operate in more than one of these trading categories simultaneously. This can work well, but only as part of a predetermined strategy.

Trading failures

Despite the available opportunities, traders often fail. They may keep failing. In the UK stock market correction of early 2000, I know of some traders who lost money they could not afford to be without. One of these had to sell his house to cover his losses.

These traders became bitter, and determined not to venture back into the stock market for a long time, if ever. Where had they gone wrong?

Seven mistakes that traders make

- Not selling fast enough. Over-optimistic traders expect that a soaring stock will always go that bit higher. They feel immobilized when the stock slips back. They are unwilling to sell out at this point, as it would mean crystallizing a loss. This would be negligible in size compared with if they sold out later, should the stock have continued to trend down.
- Relying too much on fundamentals. On a day-to-day basis, unlike in the medium-to-long term, stocks do not move mainly on fundamentals. They move because of mass buying and selling, which is largely based on sentiment, and you should trade on this basis. It is a truism that the biggest movers are often overvalued stocks.
- Using the wrong trading system. Many traders have not developed their own trading system. Instead, they make the mistake of copying others. But every trader is unique, and what works for one may not for another.
- Having too many eggs in one basket. Some traders invest a very high proportion of their available capital on one trade. This is a mistake as even the most likely winning trade can go wrong.
- Paying too much attention to Internet message boards. Traders who follow message boards can be misled by biased recommendations to buy or sell stock.
- Using inferior equipment. Serious traders who lack access to streaming share prices and fast intra-day charts are at a disadvantage.
- Thinking it is easy. Some traders treat share trading more like a hobby than a job. This is a serious mistake as they are competing against professionals. As a trader you need to commit your time

and energy to watching the markets properly, and applying proven rules.

The anatomy of failure

These are not the only mistakes that share traders make, but they are in my experience the main ones. Failed traders, like other failed business people, are viewed with horror in the UK. Unlike in the United States, we are reluctant to see the educational value of trial and error.

In the November 1997 issue of *Technically Speaking*, the newsletter of the Market Technicians Association, Dr Van K Sharp, wrote an article: 'Why it's so difficult for most people to make money on the market'. He argued: 'Most of us grew up exposed to an educational system that brainwashes us with the idea that you have to get 94%–95% correct to be excellent... Mistakes are severely punished in the school system by ridicule and poor grades, yet it is only through mistakes that human beings learn'.

Despite this, traders should not make more mistakes than they have to, as it can work out expensive. As trader Robert P Rotella said in *The Elements of Successful Trading* (New York Institute of Finance, 1992): 'Losing money when you begin trading is the price paid in learning how to trade and enter the business. But do not be misled into thinking the higher the tuition paid, the better the education'.

Most share traders gain their learning experience as novice traders from home. This is ideal for some, and it means that you can get on with other things when the markets are too choppy for trading. However, it can also lead to distractions when you should have your eye on the markets.

Position yourself in the market

Your trading base

If you are trading from home, try to set up a dedicated office, with telephone, computer and any other screens. Keep filing facilities, newspapers and other relevant reading matter to hand.

In the last four years or so, many private share traders in the United States have operated from day trading centres. This has come at a price, but the advantages are immense. The hardware available is advanced, the on-site technical support invaluable and, most importantly for some, the traders work in company. The downside is that spending all day at a day trading centre encourages over-trading.

Day trading centres have at last reached the UK. In April 2001, the first European trading room was opened in London. This offered trading in all US equity markets without the need to go through a broker. Traders using this centre had to prove they had a minimum £40,000 to invest. At the time of writing, other day trading centres are expected to open in the UK, some catering for less experienced traders.

Cultivate self-discipline

Once you have your trading base, you need to prepare yourself psychologically. To buy, hold and sell shares at suitable times looks easy in theory. In practice, it is very difficult. If you are a novice trader, fear and greed are bound to get a grip on you. When a stock has risen to a comfortable profit level, you will want to hold on to the shares to make more money. Conversely, when a share is falling, you will also want to hold on in the hope of a reversal. In both cases, you should usually do the opposite.

In the face of the various temptations, you must apply self-discipline, buying and selling when conditions are right, and not just when you *hope* to make money. To maximize your chances of success, you will also need adequate tools at your disposal. One of the most basic is Internet access.

The online advantage

Financial Web sites

Watch financial news flow as world events will affect your trading decisions. Coverage is available on Web sites such as Bloomberg (www.bloomberg.co.uk), Ample (www.ample.com), Motley Fool (www.fool.co.uk) and Citywire (www.citywire.co.uk).

On some of these sites, you can also place your trades, as well as build and watch your portfolio. You will have access to fundamental research, charts and message boards.

For the most up to date news coverage, use a Reuters or Bloomberg terminal. These are not cheap to access, but are the best options for dedicated traders.

Choose a suitable broker

Browser-based or active trader brokers

On Day 2, we examined the distinction between browser-based brokers and active trader brokers. For share traders, your choice between these two options becomes crucial. If you trade only occasionally, the browser-based broker will suit your needs.

If you are a more prolific trader, you will need the faster service of an active trader broker. The firm may require a minimum number of trades per month from you, but may charge low commissions. See the Appendix for a list of suitable brokers in both categories.

Place your order

Limit orders give you more control than market orders

On Day 2, I advised you to use a limit order when you buy or sell shares online. As a trader using a browser-based broker, this becomes essential. This is because you will be exploiting sometimes small price changes, and so cannot afford to risk the price turning against you.

If you are using an active trader broker, or otherwise have access to Level 11, you can place a market order with less risk. You will have received enough information to assess the impact on your deal from others in the queue.

Profitable share trading is harder than it appears

You will need significant returns on share trading to make it worthwhile. This is to overcome the spread and, on share purchases, stamp duty. Do not underestimate the task. In a recent seven month study, the North American Securities Association found that 70 per cent of day traders lose money.

General trading principles

Develop your own system

Share trading is a game, and money is the way you keep the score. The way to succeed is to develop a system that works for you. Using the principles in this book as a basis, this system could involve *any* combination of fundamental and technical analysis that gets you results.

Once you have a system in place, fine-tune it. Do not abandon it to suit particular trading circumstances, or it will not function as a system at all. Likewise, your system will not work if you are unduly influenced by the share tips of others. Nor will you succeed if you play the markets half-heartedly.

Once you have developed your trading system, you should become so practised at using it that the process becomes automatic.

Remember too that all share traders need breaks from their work. When you find that you are not concentrating on the market, and are missing out on potential gains, take time out. Even if it is just for a day or two, you will come back to your work refreshed.

Protect your trading capital

Only trade with capital that you can afford to lose. In her online column for rookie traders (www.onlinetradingacademy.com), guru Toni Turner has gone so far as to suggest that traders should shout to themselves throughout the trading day: 'Protect my principal'.

The warning is particularly applicable if you are approaching retirement age. Do not at this point trade with your life savings. As renowned US trader Ed Seycota said, 'There are old traders and there are bold traders, but there are very few old, bold traders'.

Diversify your risk

As a rule of thumb, do not expose more than 25 per cent of your entire trading capital to losses. This way, if you were to sell your positions at any time, you should always have 75 per cent of your trading capital in place.

In addition, do not invest more than 15 per cent of your capital on any single share trade. This way, if one trade fails, it will not affect most of your capital.

If in doubt, stay out

If you are having a run of unsuccessful trades, stop. As legendary share trader William Gann wrote in *How to Make Profits in Commodities*: 'When you make one to three trades that show losses, whether they be large or small, something is wrong with you and not the market. Your trend may have changed. My rule is to get out and wait. Study the reason for your losses.'

When you should buy

Buy only for a reason

You should always have a good reason for buying a stock. This might be on good news. If, for instance, the company has just jumped a regulatory hurdle, enabling it to launch a favoured new product, the share price should react favourably. The trick is to buy early enough, but not before the upward movement of the share price has been confirmed.

If a stock is doing well, you may want to pyramid your position. This way, you will keep buying the stock in stages, although never in so large a quantity as the previous time.

Winners and losers

At some popular financial Web sites such as Ample (www.ample.com), you will find details on the day's biggest winners and losers. Early in the morning, it can be profitable to invest in yesterday's losers, as well as in stocks that have just started rising.

Buy proven high-flyers

Buy shares that have relative strength, which implies a strong price performance over the last month or two or last year compared with other companies in the sector (see Day 5). In such cases, the PE ratio is likely to be high.

You can calculate relative strength as follows. Divide the price of your chosen share by the figure of the Actuaries All-Share index at close of business, and the result is the relative strength ratio. Recalculate this ratio every day over some months, and plot the line on a graph. If the line is moving up, so is the share's relative strength, and *vice versa*.

Buy liquid stocks

Buy stocks that are liquid, which means easily bought and sold. These are shares in large companies as they have the narrowest spreads, and the most trading volume. These days, many large companies are sufficiently volatile to make traders money.

When the share price rises, it must obviously cover the spread and your entire dealing costs before you start making a paper profit.

When you should sell

When you buy a stock, set its selling level

At the time of buying your stock, set the percentage rise at which you plan to sell it. You will learn by experience the best rate for you.

Some traders bank a significant number of gains throughout the day on very small movements in share prices. This way, they hold a stock over a period of perhaps several weeks, but are in and out of it several times in a day.

Cut your losses

Adapting Pareto's principle, 80 per cent of your profits will come from just 20 per cent of your trades. This is close to the mark, provided that you cut your losses and run your profits, as you should always do.

This means that, if the shares are going down, get out, even if there is no company-specific reason for the decline. Do not try to fight the market. If your shares are rising fast, there is a school of thought that you should sell half your position to lock in a certain profit.

A stop loss limits your risk

Be sure to use a stop loss. It could save you a fortune in the long run. The simplest type is the conventional stop loss. Under this, if the shares fall a given percentage below the original purchase price, you will automatically sell out. Occasionally, the shares will fall too fast to get out in time, in which case you should do so at a price as close as possible to your stop.

Better still, you can use the trailing stop loss. This form of stop loss trails the share price. If the share price falls a given percentage from the previous day's level achieved, you will automatically sell out.

Do not set your stop loss percentage too low. In choppy markets, the share price may fluctuate so much that, if you used only a 10 per cent stop loss, you would be closing out on the first temporary dips. Instead, you could ride these by using a 15 per cent, 20 per cent or 25 per cent stop loss. One share trader of my acquaintance fails to make money precisely because he sells out of winning stocks too quickly, on the basis of a narrow stop loss.

Never extend or eliminate the stop loss to avoid taking a small loss, as it may then grow into a large one. Do not be fooled by experienced traders who boast that they never use a stop loss. Most will sell out quickly if the stock starts plummeting, and so are applying the discipline in all but name.

Learn more about trading

Reading and surfing

On Day 12, I recommend some of the best books on share trading. Also explore relevant Web sites. One of my favourites is Career DayTrader.com (www.careerdaytrader.com), which has useful educational articles, and interviews with traders. Also visit DayTraders.com (www.daytraders.com), which has advice on trading strategies. You will find similarly valuable advice at trader Robert Miner's Web site (www.dynamictraders.com).

If you want a laugh, visit one of the various financial astrology Web sites for traders. They flourish because so many traders are superstitious and seek a rational explanation for market fluctuations when there is none.

Hands-on trading courses

The Internet will inform you of the many hands-on trading courses on offer at any given time. Some are duds. What counts is the quality of the trainer. If you are learning from a successful trader, this can be money well spent.

I note that Martin Cole, a professional investor, offers a four-day course in trading futures, mainly in the German DAX index, on the Costa del Sol. He teaches a low risk strategy, and trades live in front of students, which is a strong recommendation. Details are on Cole's Web site (www.learningtotrade.com).

Neuro-linguistic programming (NLP)

Some share traders who get easily carried away by emotion have gained from neuro-linguistic programming (NLP). The method is based on studies of excellence in human behaviour and language that Richard Bandler and John Grindler conducted in California in 1972.

NLP – dubbed 'software for the brain' – works on the principle that a committed novice trader can learn the techniques of a more experienced mentor. To achieve this, the novice trader needs *toward* motivation, in which he or she foresees a positive outcome, and *away* motivation, to protect against too much risk. These are combined with related visualization techniques.

Simulated trading

As we saw on Day 2, some brokers offer fantasy trading facilities. As a variation on the theme, HSX provides those who register with its site (www.hsx.com) with free experience of a virtual stock market online. You will invest mock Hollywood dollars in films and film stars, aiming to buy low and sell high.

The way forward

If you plan on succeeding in share trading, the rewards can be great but do not expect an easy ride. In his classic poem 'If', Rudyard Kipling wrote:

> If you can make one heap of all your winnings
> And risk it on one turn of pitch-and-toss
> And lose, and start again at your beginnings
> And never breathe a word about your loss
> Yours is the Earth and everything that's in it
> And – which is more – you'll be a Man, my son!

This has been the apprenticeship of every successful trader. Soon it will be your turn. However, do not start trading until you have read this book. Beyond what you have covered to date, it is important that you have a grasp of technical analysis (Day 5), options and warrants (Day 9), and futures and spread betting (Day 10). Remember that *learning* about trading is your first step towards the *practice* of it.

Dynamic rules of the Online Share Buyer's FlexiSystem

- As a trader, you must be independent, logical, decisive and self-disciplined.
- If you are trading from home, try to set up a dedicated office.
- Take a small loss early to avoid a potentially large one later.
- As a trader, do not buy and sell only on fundamentals.
- Develop your own trading system.
- Only trade with capital that you can afford to lose, and do not invest too much on any single trade.
- If you are scared, this is good as it can make you trade more carefully.

- If you trade much, use an active trader broker, or Level 11 quotes.
- If you trade shares through a browser-based broker, use limit orders.
- Day trading centres provide good hardware, technical support, and the company of fellow traders, but are expensive and may tempt you to over-trade.
- Take breaks from share trading, particularly when it is going badly.
- Only buy for a good reason, and favour liquid stocks that have relative strength.
- Use a stop loss. Do not set it too low, and do not extend it in the throes of trading.

Day 5
How technical analysis can make you money

Overview

Technical analysis – the interpreting and forecasting of share price and market movements through indicators and charts – is unreliable. But as some major players use technical analysis, it influences markets. For this reason, it pays you to understand the principles.

In this module, we will first take a look at the pros and cons of technical analysis, and set it in context. Next, you will have an exciting crash course in the basics of this complex (some would say convoluted) subject. The emphasis will be on how you can make practical use of charting in your investment decisions.

We will start with Dow theory, and proceed to compare the different types of chart in popular use, including the esoteric Japanese candlesticks. We will look at how to plot these charts, and how to interpret them. You will find here a clear explanation of such basic concepts as support and resistance, fan lines, trend penetration, and volume.

We will define and discuss continuation patterns such as the triangle and flag, and reversal patterns such as the head and shoulders, and double top. Technical indicators such as Bollinger bands and stochastics will come under scrutiny. We will glance at Fibonacci ratios and Elliot Wave theory before we end the course with suggestions for useful further research and computerized charting programs.

The theory of technical analysis

How technical analysis works

Online investors have found that value investing works well over a period but not in the short term. For trading and short term investing situations in particular, some have wished to develop their skill at buying and selling shares on the basis of price movements. For this, they have found technical analysis relevant, and it is enjoying a boom in popularity.

Technical analysis involves analysing charts and various indicators to forecast future share price and index movements. At its most basic, these charts and indicators provide a visual summary of the perpetual conflict between buyers and sellers in the market, which manifests itself in share price fluctuations.

The technical analyst claims to be able to reach conclusions from seeing the share price movements, but without knowing the reasons. He studies the effect and not the cause. This way, he aims to complement rather than counteract the fundamental analyst, who sees share price movements ultimately reflecting the value of the underlying company.

The problem with technical analysis is that past share price and market movements may not repeat themselves in the same form, on the same time scale. The old adage still goes round the City: 'I have never seen a rich technician'.

This is misleading, as there are some outstanding equity investors who have based investment decisions largely on technical analysis. US share trader Marty Schwartz used fundamental analysis for nine years, and it did not work well. He switched to using technical analysis and became rich. US fund manager William O'Neil, another enthusiast, said: 'Just as a doctor would be foolish not to use X-rays and EKGs, investors would be foolish not to use charts'.

Many other great investors are not convinced. Undeniably, the charts and indicators provide usefully accessible information about past share price movements. There is no documented evidence that these past movements may be used to predict the future.

What is clear is that it is possible to earn a living forecasting on the basis of the charts, and writing and lecturing about technical analysis. Some technical analysts flatter the undiscriminating by saying that they can win at the investment game through a knowledge of crowd psychology. This initiates a great feeling of superiority. Also, if enough people trade or invest on the basis of technical analysis, it becomes a self-fulfilling prophecy.

Given the variables, technical analysis is more of an art than a science. It is least applicable to companies with no track record and unpredictable share price movements, such as those in the high-tech sector. Technical analysts agree that their craft works better if several technical charts and indicators point to the same outcome. It also helps if there is fundamental support.

The basis of technical analysis

Technical analysts dispute the finer points of their craft, but are agreed on the basics. A share price moves in trends. Once started, a trend perpetuates itself. The art of technical analysis is to pinpoint a possible trend change early and, if it is confirmed, to recommend action.

Once a trend has started, it will continue for an unpredictable period. A clearly defined reverse signal indicates that the trend may be coming to an end. As a technical analyst, you look only for probabilities.

The Dow Theory

Much of what we know about trends is derived from the so-called Dow Theory, which evolved from the original researches of financial journalist Charles Dow who died in 1902.

In 1897, Dow developed two stock market indices: The Industrial Average, which consisted of 12 blue-chip companies, and The Rail Average, which included 20 railroad companies. He studied these as a way to gauge business conditions, but was not involved in the forecasting of stock prices. Dow's successor, William Hamilton, developed these findings, and created an early version of what is now known as the Dow theory. In 1932 a formal version of this was published.

According to Dow theory, the share price reflects everything that is known about a stock. This is an early version of the so-called efficient market hypothesis (see Day 1). In addition, there are always three trends in the stock market: primary, secondary and tertiary.

The primary or main trend in a market or stock lasts for at least a year. In the early stage of a primary trend, a few informed investors buy in advance of economic recovery. Next, economic conditions recover, and a majority buy. Finally, the economy is booming and there is the biggest rush to buy, but informed investors are selling. The primary trend is interrupted intermittently by a secondary trend, lasting one to three months, which typically retraces between a third and two thirds of the gain or loss. There is also the tertiary or minor trend, which lasts from one day to three weeks, and is unimportant.

According to Dow theory, a primary trend confirmed by the two given indices will continue until its reversal has been firmly signalled. There must be confirmation of a change in trend from more than one signal.

Trading volumes go with the trend, increasing as the price rises, and falling as the price declines, under Dow theory. If the share price moves up or down on the back of rising volume, it is likely to hold. This is because the movement is backed by buying and selling from a large number of individuals. Conversely, if the share price moves up or down on declining volume, only a small number of buyers or sellers will have set the price. The trend may not continue.

Different kinds of chart

As a technical analyst, you may use any of these five main types of chart.

Bar chart

This is a popular chart which gives the technician a lot of information instantly. In this chart, the share price or index level is plotted against price on a Y (vertical) axis and time on an X (horizontal) axis. A bar is drawn for each day (or other time period) used in the chart.

Each bar for a given day shows the high and low share prices. A tick on the left of the bar shows the opening price, and a tick on the right shows the closing price.

Line chart

This chart provides less information than a bar chart, but is more useful for charting long-term trends. It has a line that plots only the closing price against time. On the Y axis you will find price, and on the X axis you will find time.

The most usual price to be plotted is the closing mid-price, in which case the 'noise' of intra-day ups and downs in the share price, which you get on a bar chart, is eliminated. This way, it becomes easier to spot trend changes.

The line chart shows prices over a period of your choice. This could be every five minutes or, otherwise, daily, weekly or fortnightly.

Point-and-figure chart

The point-and-figure chart shows even less information than a line chart. This way, however, it cuts out still more 'noise' of detail, focusing even further on trends. Among fans is London-based technical analysis guru David Fuller.

In the point-and-figure chart, the Y axis represents price, and the X axis measures time on an irregular basis, with prices being plotted only when a significant and pre-decided change has taken place.

Let us suppose that 10p is the required level of change on a point-and-figure chart representing a stock price. In this example, every time that the share price rises by 10p on a point-and-figure chart representing a stock price, an X will be marked. When the price falls by 10p, an 0 will marked. In either case, if the movement marks a break from previous rises or falls, it will be in a new column. Sideways trading, involving insignificant share price changes, is ignored.

On computer-generated charts, upward-pointing chevrons may be used for price rises, and downwards-pointing chevrons for price falls.

Candlesticks

These are an exotic area of technical analysis which originated in the Far East. In recent years, they have become popular with share traders in the West. They provide broadly similar information to bar charts but, for advanced users, have an extra intuitive element.

On a chart, the candlestick has a vertical line that extends from the high to the low of the share price. One horizontal line crosses the vertical line at the underlying stock's opening price, and another at its closing price.

These two horizontal lines are joined up on either side, creating a vertical rectangle known as a real body. When the closing price was higher than at opening, the real body is transparent, and in the reverse case, it is black.

Equivolume

The theory behind equivolume charts is that *volume* rather than *time* influences price changes. The charts include price and volume in a single, two-dimensional box, the width of which is determined by volume. The top line of the box represents the highest price reached, and the bottom line the lowest.

How to plot the charts

Using computers and plotting by hand

If you want to become your own technical analyst, you should get used to plotting share price index movements over your chosen time period on a chart. This is where computers can help you. With the right software package, the computer will do all the work for you instantly.

However, some technical analysts insist on drawing their most important charts by hand as this forces them to pay extra attention to the detail. When you are starting out, you could do worse than follow their example.

Investment is a percentage game. As a rule of thumb, draw your charts on logarithmically scaled paper, where the square gets increasingly small as you move up the paper in line with percentage gains, rather than on arithmetically scaled paper where the square stays the same size in line with absolute gains.

How to use the charts

The trend is your friend

As an investor, you should 'go with the flow'. In this case, the flow refers to the trend lines of a share price or index that appear on your chart. An up-trend line connects rising market bottoms, while a down-trend line connects falling market highs.

An up-trend in the share price shows that demand is greater than supply, and you should buy the shares for as long as it lasts. Conversely, if the trend is down, you should sell the shares or go short on them, again until the trend reverses. If the share price stays within a trading range, it is as a result of demand and supply being roughly balanced.

The longer a trend lasts, the more reliable it is likely to be. Trends remain until they are broken – at which point relevant software packages will trigger off alarms.

Resistance and support

The resistance level represents the top price level to which a share or index may rise. At this point, sellers become strong enough to stop buyers from continuing to force up the share price.

Conversely, the support level is the bottom price level to which a share or index may fall. Here, buyers become strong enough to stop the share price falling further.

The faster the share price has moved in advance, the more significant is the resistance or support level. Similarly, the more often the level is *tested*, the more reliable it is.

In practice, support and resistance levels are often at a round number, as this seems a natural entry point for buyers and sellers.

Trend channels

Once a trend has three tops or bottoms in line – enabling a line to be drawn against the three points that confirm the trend – it is far more certain.

A trend channel is the area between the trend line that touches the highest points on the chart and indicates resistance, and a return line running parallel that touches the lowest points and indicates support. In this way, the trend channel is sandwiched between the trend line and the return line.

If the stock is volatile, its trend channel will be large enough to enable you to buy and sell profitably on price fluctuations within the channel. Before you do this, divide the trend channel along the middle with a horizontal line. When the share price is above this dividing line, it is your cue to sell the underlying shares, and when it is below, this is your cue to buy them.

Fan lines

If the tops or bottoms of share price movements on your chart are not in line, you can draw separate lines defining two possible trends. The first line will be from the first top or bottom to the second. The second line will be from the second top or bottom to the third. Once these lines are three in number, they are called fan lines. After a third fan line has been found, a trend will often be reversed.

Penetration of trend

Once the share price has broken a trend – climbing above the resistance level or below the support level – this is known as penetration of the trend. Penetration of the support level will happen usually for a significant reason such as a profit warning or dividend reduction, and will often be substantial.

If the break out is above the resistance line, this level becomes a support. Similarly, if the market falls below a support line, that level becomes a resistance.

A trading tip

Here is a tip. Think about buying or selling as soon as possible *after* penetration of the trend. The reversal, if it is *bona fide*, is likely to be sharp. To increase the odds in your favour, make your move when the penetration seems major, and is accompanied by heavy volume.

Volume

You will often find volume displayed at the bottom of charts in the form of vertical bars. Sometimes, volume is shown in a separate chart.

Either way, the display is usually on a relative adjusted volume basis, with the bottom of the bars showing the lowest volume traded, rather than none. This way, you can more easily spot uncharacteristic trends in volume.

We will now take a look at chart patterns. These are controversial and some technical analysts do not believe in them. They may be broadly divided into continuation and reversal patterns.

Chart patterns

Continuation patterns

Continuation patterns indicate that the share price will continue in the direction that it had been taking before the pattern started. They *confirm* the trend.

The triangle

The triangle is a common but not always reliable continuation pattern. It is formed from a zig-zag pattern in the shape of a triangle dwindling into a point. This triangle represents a battle between buyers and sellers.

Eventually, either the buyers or the sellers win, and the price breaks free of the triangle. Measure the depth of the triangle at the start, and use this length as the target for the initial rise or fall of the share price, once it breaks out.

The more often the share price touches the side of the triangle which encloses it, the more reliable is the pattern. If it is a right-angled triangle, it is seen as more reliable than if it is symmetrical.

The rectangle

The rectangle appears less often than the triangle but is arguably a more reliable predictor. It is formed from a zigzag pattern on a line chart that takes the form of a rectangle in which the temporary battle between buyers and sellers is clearly seen.

The rectangle will typically last for months, until the share price breaks through either its bottom line – representing support; or its top line – representing resistance. The gap between these two lines represents your target share price movement following the break-out.

The flag

The flag is a brief consolidation in the share price that lasts up to a few weeks. It follows a sharp rise that resembles a flagpole. To detect a flag, it is easiest if you have plotted a spaciously scaled chart.

The length of the rise within the flagpole before the flag occurs is your target price movement following the break-out from the pattern.

Reversal patterns

Reversal patterns indicate that a trend is changing. This will typically happen when a bull or bear market is coming to an end. Here are some of the most common patterns.

Head and shoulders

The head and shoulders is a bearish signal. The patterns starts where the share price on the chart trends upwards to a first shoulder, then drops back completing its shape. It rises again to a new high, then drops back, so forming the head. It rises once more, but can only form another shoulder before falling down and breaking the support level, which is known as the neckline.

From this point, your minimum target for the share price to fall should be the distance as measured between the top of the head and the neckline.

There is also a reverse head and shoulders, with a similar measuring technique. This is a bullish reversal signal that is believed likely to come at the end of a bear market.

Double top or bottom

The double top is another bearish pattern, and is quite rare. Here the share price rises, and drops back, then returns to its old peak and back again. The pattern resembles two humps on a camel's back. It develops usually over some months.

The difference between the peak price of the double top and the support level – again known as the neckline – is the measure that you will use for your minimum target price, once the share price has broken out of the double top.

The double bottom is a double top in reverse. This is a bullish pattern.

Saucer top or bottom

The saucer top is more rounded than the head and shoulders or double top, and it occurs in tired bull markets. It shows the share price rise, turn slowly and reverse into decline, tracing the beginnings of a circular motion on the graph.

We will now turn our attention to some indicators used in technical analysis. These aim to enable you to improve the timing of your investments.

Technical indicators

Moving averages

When you are keeping a chart of indices or share prices, watch moving averages. These represent changes in the *average* share price over a given period.

If you were to calculate a moving average manually, you would add up the prices included in the given number of latest days. You would do this by daily adding on a price for the latest day and dropping that of the last day in the series. You would then divide the total of the prices in this updated series by the number of prices included.

If, for example, you have 20 prices on a daily basis, you would create a 20-day moving average, which would be highly sensitive given the short time period over which the average is taken. This would be suitable for keeping track of short-term investments.

If you had a 200-day moving average, this would be less volatile due to the evening out of the averages taken over the longer period. It would be suitable for keeping track of long-term investments.

Some technical analysts advise you to buy shares at a price below the moving averages. On this basis, top trader Marty Schwartz suggests that moving averages work *better than any other investment timing tool at his disposal*.

Conversely, you should sell when the moving average starts to dip. In January 2001, technicians advised this of high-flying Matalan when the quoted discount retailer broke its 200-day moving average on substantial trading volume. The following day, the share price started to fall and, three days later, a profit warning followed.

Golden and dead crosses

Keep two moving averages for your chosen index or stock running together, of which one is short term (10, 20 or 30 days) and the other long term (up to 200 days).

The short-term moving average will indicate changes before the long-term one. If the two moving averages cross over on your chart, and are both moving upwards, this is a golden cross, which is a bullish sign. Conversely, if the two moving averages cross over as they are both moving downwards, this is a dead cross, and it is a bearish sign.

In either case, the move is stronger if it is backed by substantial trading volume. Golden and dead cross signs are not always reliable. You should use these signs in particular only in conjunction with other charts or indicators.

Envelopes

An envelope consists of two moving averages. These represent the boundaries of a share's trading range. If the share price touches the upper band, it has gone too high, and this is a sell signal. If it touches the lower band, it has fallen too far and this is a buy signal.

Bollinger bands

One of the most popular types of envelope is Bollinger bands, a concept invented by John Bollinger. These are plotted at standard deviation (a volatility measure) levels above and below a moving average. They tighten when the share price is static and bulge when the share price movements become more volatile. When the share price moves outside the bands, this trend is likely to continue.

The Coppock indicator

The original Coppock principle – conceived of by Edward Coppock – is another indicator based on moving averages. It operates on the basis that if investors have made big losses, they *wait* before they return the market. The Coppock Guide, as it was named in 1962, shows a long 10-month weighted moving average. The indicator oscillates around a zero or datum line, and if it rises above this, it is a *buy* signal. There was no rule about selling.

This worked well as a predictor for the Dow Jones Industrial Average when backdated to post-war years, and throughout the 1960s and 1970s. In the UK, the magazine *Investors Chronicle* successfully applied an adapted version of the Coppock Guide retrospectively to the FT-SE 100.

In the 1980s, the Coppock Guide stopped working so well, partly because it sometimes stayed above the zero line too long. This led to related indicators being invented. *Investors Chronicle* still publishes an adapted form of monthly IC Coppock indicator for various markets.

Overbought and oversold indicators

Overbought and oversold indicators show when the market is oversold, meaning that it has fallen too far, or when the market is overbought, meaning that it has risen too far.

Relative strength indicator

There is a relative strength indicator, invented by US-based J Welles Wilder Jr, which measures when a share price is overbought and oversold. For this indicator, 50 is the neutral figure on a 1–100 scale, with 70 being overbought and 30 being oversold.

As we saw on Day 4, past relative strength – when a stock has done better than its sector or the market – is a proven indicator of likely continued out-performance. Star US share trader David Ryan regards relative strength as more important than earnings per share.

Stochastics

Stochastics are an oscillator that indicates when a share, sector or index is overbought or oversold. In this way, the oscillator is seen as heralding the future direction of the share price in the opposite direction.

The stochastic oscillator is plotted as two lines. These are the %D line (a dotted line in most software), which is based on the daily high, low and closing price over perhaps 10 or 20 days, and the %K line, which is a moving average of %D.

These lines oscillate between the extremes of 1–100 on an appropriately scaled chart. It is a *buy* signal when either of the lines falls below 25 then rises above it. Conversely, when the line goes over 75, then falls back, it is a *sell* signal. If the moving average (%K) falls below the price line (%D), this can be another *sell* signal.

You can also check whether a market is overbought or oversold by drawing a chart with a moving average that represents the market. If the market diverges much from this without a good reason, it is likely that it is becoming overbought or oversold, and it may stay that way for a while.

Advanced theories

Reintracements

Some ideas in technical analysis are based on the Fibonacci ratios, which were the brainchild of Leonardo Fibonacci, an eccentric mathematician who lived in Italy 800 years ago. According to his findings, a stock market trend is likely to retrace itself specifically by either 61.8 per cent, 50 per cent or 38.2 per cent.

The theory is rooted in Fibonacci's sequence of numbers in which each number equals its two predecessors added up. On this basis, the sequence reads 0, 1, 1, 2, 3, 5, 8, 13, etc. The ratio between two successive numbers in the sequence, barring the first few, is 61.8 per cent, which is known as the golden mean.

The Elliot Wave theory

The Fibonacci ratios helped to inspire technician Ralph Nelson Elliott, who published his Elliott Wave theory in 1939. In this famous theory, Elliot suggests that market cycles have an impulse wave of five parts, reaching new highs, which is followed by a corrective wave of three parts. The waves interrelate according to various rules, including the Fibonacci numbers. But problems remain in assessing where one wave starts and another finishes.

The Elliot Wave theory requires a certain amount of subjective judgement. It has its supporters and its detractors. One enthusiast is now slightly faded stock market guru Bob Beckman. He once quipped that there were only a few people besides himself who understood the Elliot Wave theory, one of whom was dead, and another of whom had forgotten it.

Further reading and research

This module has introduced the fascinating and controversial subject of technical analysis. I have deliberately not referred to some esoteric theories such as those of Gann. If you are interested, you can explore these in various more detailed studies (see Day 12).

There are plenty of newsletters, online and in hard copy form, that offer stock tips based on what the charts reveal. Many are dense in style, and do not have a good track record in giving reliable tips. I am pleased to be able to tell you of a newsletter which, although it is early days yet, appears to be an exception.

The Chart Prophet, published by Fleet Street Publications, has made some excellent tips based on the charts, and instructs you about technical analysis as you go along. Unlike many of its competitors across the globe, it is written in a very reader-friendly way, and is accessible to beginners. At the time of writing, there have been only a few issues published, so time will tell how the tips will really work out, but this looks to me a promising project.

Online there are a great many resources for active or passive technicians. For excellent definitions and explanations spanning technical analysis, visit the Web site of Technical Analysis from A to Z (www.equis.com/free/taaz).

For practical purposes, you will find a fantastic charting facility at FTMarketWatch (www.ftmarketwatch.com). Here, you can pull up a chart of your favourite company and compare its share price performance with the market. You will also have access to more sophisticated charting functions, including moving averages.

I would also recommend the technical analysis service at Ample (www.ample.com). If the bug bites hard and you want to draw your own trendlines, use the AIQ charts in the mytrack program (www.mytrack.com).

Consider too obtaining professional charting programs, which offer real-time share prices and significant charting flexibility. The message board on financial Web sites will give some useful pointers on which might be best for you. Some programs such as Omnitrader (www.omnitrader.com) put stocks through technical analysis hoops to select the most promising investment propositions. Otherwise, the leading UK programs include Synergy (www.synergy.com), Updata (www.updata.com) and Indexia (www.indexia.co.uk).

The way forward

Technical analysis is fun, but it is not always reliable. I hate to spoil the party, folks, but I know of plenty of investors who have lost fortunes following technical analysis blindly. Do not join them. If you get hooked on technical analysis, use fundamental analysis as well, and err on the side of caution.

Dynamic rules of the Online Share Buyer's FlexiSystem

- Technical analysis is based on the flawed premise that past share price and market movements repeat themselves.

- When enough people invest on the basis of technical analysis, it becomes a self-fulfilling prophecy.
- The art of technical analysis is to pinpoint a possible trend early. The longer the trend, and the more it is backed by rising volume, the more reliable it will be.
- Buy shares at a price that is below the moving averages.
- Look for continuation patterns to confirm a trend, and reversal patterns to indicate that it is changing.
- The Elliott Wave theory is complicated, and it can be difficult to assess where one wave starts and the other finishes.
- The best tip sheet based on technical analysis is *The Chart Prophet*, published by Fleet Street Publications. In addition, there are plenty of free Web sites to keep you informed.

Day 6
How to win in the penny share casino

Overview

In this module, we will look at various types of penny stock, and how to select these for investment. We will look at the best ways to buy and sell these stocks, and at the most important markets on which they are traded.

We will see why you need to be flexible in your valuation of penny stocks, and will touch on some of the more common creative accounting techniques in use. We will look at the risks of fraud and, finally, the tax advantages of investing in unquoted companies.

In a world of their own

Penny shares can be little more than a gamble. They are the fun side of investing but, also, unfortunately, a major part of its crooked side. Other things being equal, the younger the company in which you invest, the greater the risk.

The choice of markets is large. The company may be listed on the London Stock Exchange, or instead on the Alternative Investment Market (AIM) or The Off Exchange (OFEX) market. Many stocks are listed on a market or trading facility abroad, or are not listed anywhere.

Most define a penny share by its upper price limit. In the UK, some specialist brokers require a share price of less than £1.00, while others set the ceiling at £3.00 – to include stocks that were once priced at far below this level but have subsequently risen. It is best to be flexible as some stocks trading at over £1.00 may be as risky as those trading at less.

The risks and the rewards for penny shares arise partly because they have a thin market. A stock priced at 10p may rise 50 per cent on good news, whereas an old economy blue-chip stock will not. Conversely, the penny share can fall more sharply in percentage terms than its larger cousin. The price may bear no relation to the stock's underlying value.

This is particularly so if predators show an interest in a small company. The share price can soar on speculation that there may be a contested takeover bid at a considerably higher value than the current share price. If you can buy shares in the putative target company *before* it makes its major rise, and get out before the speculation subsides, you will have made a quick killing.

For such reasons, you will not always buy penny shares on value grounds. You need to be ready to nip in and out of stocks, keeping a sharp eye on share price changes. In addition, you will find some penny shares in which it is worth investing for the longer term.

Categories of penny share

First let us look the variety of penny shares on offer.

Recovery stocks

Recovery stocks have seen better days but have fallen out of favour. They were once perhaps stock market darlings. In their present state, they have survived only because they restructured their business, perhaps lopping off unprofitable divisions, or making a synergistic acquisitions.

A recovery stock could double in value within a week, or in a few months. It is more likely to do nothing, or to decline in value. It may become a takeover target, which can turn out very profitable for the penny share speculator who has invested in it early.

A favourite type of recovery situation is the shell company. The shell is likely to be priced low, and will have little or no substantial business of its own. It will have a share structure that enables new management, perhaps already a substantial shareholder, to seize control.

If you are considering investing in a recovery company, compare the current share price to high and low prices in the past year. But bear in mind that, simply because a share has done well in the past, this does not mean that it will do so again.

Cyclical stocks

Cyclical stocks rise and fall in value with the business cycle. For example, mining and resource companies may close their operations in the winter due to bad weather, and the share price would decline to reflect this. The companies would resume activity in the spring and summer, and their share price would duly rise again. The message is clear. Sell these stocks in June, just before production subsides, and buy back in December.

Regardless of how good your timing is, you will find that many mining and resource stocks are worthless. Some bucket-shop penny share dealers specialize in selling the duds to gullible private investors. One broker boasted to me how his team raked in £2 million in a day putting private investors into an unquoted oil company that 'does not even have a hole in the ground'.

The most reliable area of cyclical investment is house-building and related activity. When the economy looks strong, invest in companies involved in these activities as they will be reaping the benefits of a housing boom.

Internet companies

As we have already pointed out, Internet companies are exceptionally volatile and have few or no tangible assets. They may rise or fall frequently by several hundred per cent within a matter of weeks. This could be for company-specific reasons, but is more often in line with the sector.

In the year or longer from March 2000, the Internet sector went from being one of the most expensive in the stock market to one of the best value. At the time of writing, you can invest in the cream of the sector cheaply. On how to value Internet companies, see Day 3.

Biotechnology companies

Young biotechnology companies are a particularly high-risk investment. Fewer than 10 per cent of their products reach clinical development, although the success rate improves as production leaps early hurdles. The risks are reflected in the aggressively high discount rates that analysts use in their DCF analysis of such companies.

When investing in early-stage biotech companies, look for a pipeline of at least several products, some of which have a large market.

New issues

To invest in new issues of penny shares is to enter the unknown. New issues are often overpriced, and allocation of shares in good companies may be limited. For more advice on this subject, see Day 7.

How to select the right penny stocks

Make your own stock selections

Ultimately you must make your own investment decisions and not rely on the help of others. Some penny share tipsters are good, but may fail you on advice about when to sell the stocks you have bought. More than a few are crooked. For an inside perspective on the fascinating world of tipsters, see Day 8.

Be flexible on valuation

When you select penny shares for investment, you must take into account that they are not subject to the usual stock valuation rules. In the short term, the level of PE ratio, for instance, will rarely make much difference. Some young companies, particularly in the Internet sector, do not even have a PE ratio as this is made up partly from earnings (see Day 3), and they have none.

If you are looking for penny shares that you are going to tuck away for some months or years, you need to pay more attention to valuation than if you are buying strictly for the short term.

Market perception

In the short term, penny share valuations are highly susceptible to fluctuating market perception. On this basis, you should invest in what is popular, sometimes taking a cue from top City fund managers – as Bruce McWilliams, editor of *Red Hot Penny Shares*, a leading penny share newsletter, advised private investors at a London conference in 2001.

McWilliams' strategy can work if you watch stock prices closely, and deal at opportune times. Try to predict rather than reflect trends in your investment trends. If, for instance, you discover that a pharmaceutical company is about to publish the results of drug tests that are expected to be good, and this is not yet reflected in the share price, invest early. If the test results meet expectations, the share price could soar.

As part of the same investment strategy, shun shares that are blatantly over-puffed. Do not suffer the fate of those investors who bought overvalued Internet stocks in late 1999 and early 2000 and failed to sell out before the market corrected itself.

The riskiest penny shares are not confined to the Internet sector. Avoid biotechnology companies that overspend on research, assuming without full justification that their early-stage products will come to the market. The market may initially give credence to these assumptions and inflate the share price. If reality proves unkind, the share price may collapse.

Check the quality of management

When you assess the management of, for instance, Internet or biotechnology companies, look for leadership as well as technological expertise. The two do not always come together. If they are wise, the technology experts who start up small high-tech companies will employ hands-on management that is experienced and capable in the areas where they are not. An example of this is Charles Muirhead, the 25-year-old technology genius, who employed experienced management to run his successful Internet software company Orchestream, which was floated on the London Stock Exchange in July 2000 (see Day 7).

In the penny share game particularly, a change in management can be the catalyst for a positive earnings surprise that will send the share price soaring. You can gain an inkling of pending staff changes either by ringing up the company and asking about its business, or from its recruitment advertising in the national press.

Look for strong asset backing

A small company will ideally have a net asset value per share that is higher than its share price (for calculating the figures, see Day 3). This will help it to survive through lean times, or worse. If a company is wound up, the liquidator will distribute to shareholders in proportion to the company's assets.

Do not look for asset backing in a young Internet company. It will have none unless perhaps it combines an established, stable bricks-and-mortar business with an Internet division poised for growth. Such a hybrid will reduce the risk for investors, but will arguably have less growth potential than a pure Internet play.

Young biotechnology companies will ideally be funded by pharmaceutical companies in return for rights to drugs under development. This reduces the risk for a biotechnology company, but also its potential return.

Accounting tricks

Creative accounting is prevalent in penny stocks. Based on manipulated accounts, a company can enhance its apparent financial status. This may fool the market for a while, but not forever.

On Day 3 we looked at the concept of annual depreciation, and how this reduces the value of a company's assets. In small companies, look for a *consistent* depreciation policy. Make sure too that depreciation is not so low that it has unrealistically minor impact on the profit and loss account every year.

In addition, be wary when an item that would normally be an expense in the profit and loss account is made an asset on the balance sheet. For instance, interest on property development loans is sometimes capitalized in this way, on the basis that it is a realistic cost of the project.

When a company's assets are bolstered by capitalized expenses, its gearing – interest bearing loans and preference share capital, divided by ordinary shareholders' funds (assets less liabilities) – will be lower. So also will be interest cover, defined as earnings per share divided by net interest payable per share. This makes the company look a better investment proposition.

The ratio modification involved is acceptable, provided that the anticipated revenues materialize. Sometimes they do not, and the capitalized expenses have to be drastically reduced. This leads to mayhem and a sharp reduction in the share price, or the collapse of the company.

A creative accounting technique which UK software companies in particular are prone to use is advance revenue recognition. This is when a company records a sale in its accounts before the customer is due to pay. It is seen as a way to compensate for providing a long credit period for customers. In the United States, companies are not allowed to do this and must recognize revenue on an incremental basis.

After you have valued penny shares, check the market in which they are traded, if any. This can make a significant difference to their profile, their liquidity and their initial and ongoing expenses.

Penny share markets

OFEX

Be cautious about investing in stocks trading on the Off Exchange (OFEX) trading facility which, in early 2001, achieved the status of a market. Some OFEX companies will only have been operating for a few months or less, and are invariably high risk. On a positive note, JP Jenkins, the sole market maker in OFEX stocks, is a highly reputable London Stock Exchange member firm.

OFEX is increasingly working as a springboard for companies looking to move onto the Alternative Investment Market (AIM) or a full listing on the London Stock Exchange. You can do well if you invest in such future stars early. The problem is how to identify them. Asking the companies themselves may not be the best method. Many will claim to be planning a higher listing. Some will have incorporated this into their original business plan. They may say that they are talking to brokers.

The reality is that most of these companies will not move on and up. Even if they do, not every such company will necessarily sustain a higher listing. Some find it hard to adjust to the resulting sudden increase in their shareholder base, and greater liquidity, leading to likely fluctuations in the share price.

Also, a higher listing does not allow the same opportunities for mistakes on the learning curve. On OFEX, a company can temporarily manage without a finance director. On the London Stock Exchange, this would be unacceptable.

If, despite the caveats, you want to invest in OFEX companies, here are some ways in which you can improve your chances of success.

Invest in large companies

As a rule of thumb, you are better off investing in large companies. It is mostly these that move from OFEX to the AIM or a full listing, according to independent surveys. Also, larger companies, other things being equal, are more resistant to problems than their smaller brethren, and are likely to have been going for longer.

Do your research

Basic research on OFEX companies is easier than you might think. Your first port of call should be the official OFEX Web site (www.ofex.com). This gives you news flow on its companies and financial data. It will also give you a company's phone number and details of its directors.

Also visit the Web site of unquoted.co.uk (www.unquoted.co.uk), a provider of comprehensive, independent news and information about OFEX companies. Look up details of a company there. Read interviews with company directors. Use the message boards, where investors will communicate with each other with a sometimes disarming frankness.

Talk to management

Before you invest in an OFEX company, it is useful to talk to its key management. Ring up companies and ask politely for the chief executive officer or finance director by name. Because these companies are small, such key individuals are often personally available on the phone, and extremely helpful. If the individual involved is not available, he or she will often return your call later. Before phoning, have some questions ready – about what the company does, its plans and its financials – but be prepared to stray into related areas.

Try to attend one of the excellent OFEX conferences held in various parts of the UK throughout the year (details on the OFEX Web site). Here the management of companies – which may be a bunch of people in their early thirties – will explain their business, and give out brochures. They will sometimes give presentations. Also, lawyers, accountants, consultants, fund managers and others peripherally involved in OFEX will chat with you for free.

Do not invest on the basis of sector

OFEX stocks are largely immune from the trends that affect the mainstream markets. If Nasdaq falls 50 per cent over a few months, high-tech stocks on the London Stock Exchange are likely to follow suit, but OFEX stocks will not. As in other markets, they will, however, fluctuate for company-specific reasons.

Where to deal

It is possible to deal in OFEX stocks through your stockbroker. Some brokers may advise you to avoid OFEX as a market that is too small for institutional investors and so lacks liquidity. Others are more enthusiastic.

In early 2001, a dedicated online OFEX dealing service was launched. This was Equities Direct (www.equities-direct.co.uk). The service is a trading name of JP Jenkins and is provided by Barclays Stockbrokers. Through this service, you can not only deal in OFEX shares online, but can also get free up-to-date prices.

Otherwise, in the *Financial Times* and the London *Evening Standard* you can follow the prices of those OFEX shares that have paid to list there.

AIM

Unlike OFEX, the AIM was created, and is regulated by the London Stock Exchange. It was launched in 1995 to meet the needs of small growing companies. By early 2001, there were more than 535 companies quoted on the AIM, and over £6.3 billion had been raised on it. More than 70 companies have progressed from the AIM to the main market.

Companies on the AIM are regulated less than those that are fully listed on the London Stock Exchange, which is particularly helpful if they make acquisitions. Also, companies will have had less stringent entry requirements. For a full listing, a three-year trading record is required (with some exceptions) and 25 per cent of shares must be in public hands. On the AIM, these rules do not apply.

Further information

For up-to-date information on the AIM, visit the Web site of the London Stock Exchange (www.londonstockexchange.com). You can see here an online slide-show about the AIM, as well as further details of constituent companies. There are some AIM company profiles including, at the time of writing, that of EpicGroup, the online training and e-business solutions group.

You will also find on this site a useful brochure about the AIM that you can download as a PDF format file. Although this is mostly for companies considering listing, it has case studies that are of interest to the investor, including one of health club group Fitness First, and how an AIM listing helped to fund its expansion.

If you have further questions, the London Stock Exchange offers an AIM helpline (020 7797 4404). You might also visit the Web site of Newsletter Publishing Ltd (www.redsky.com) which offers a free sample of the AIM Newsletter, which has useful coverage of choice stocks for private investors. In addition, go to the Web site of BDO Stoy Hayward (www.bdo.co.uk) which provides a brief history of the AIM.

For dealing purposes, check out the user-friendly Web site of Graham H Wills & Company (www.ghw.co.uk), an independent financial adviser and stockbroker that specializes in offering IPOs in OFEX and AIM companies. The site explains such matters as tax relief for AIM investments, and enables you to request (and download) prospectuses.

The TechMARK index.

The rules for a full listing can be relaxed for companies that are quoted on the volatile FTSE TechMARK All share index. Qualifying companies must have a low minimum market capitalization (share price × number of shares in issue) of £50 million, and must provide quarterly annual reports. They do not need a three-year track record.

These companies must depend on technological innovation for their success. Qualifying companies in computer hardware, computer services, the Internet, semiconductors, software and telecoms equipment are included automatically on TechMARK, and others are included where relevant.

Further details

For further details on the TechMARK index, go to the relevant part of the London Stock Exchange Web site (www.londonstockexchange.com/techmark), or call the help line 020 7797 2000. For further information on this and other indices, visit www.ftse.com. National newspapers that follow the TechMARK index include the *Financial Times*, *The Daily Telegraph*, *Mail on Sunday* and *The Guardian*.

US markets

If you want to buy penny stocks in the United States, check that they are fully listed, probably on Nasdaq. Unless you know what you are doing, avoid stocks quoted on the US-based National Quotation Bureau's Pink Sheets, or the OTC Bulletin Board. The stocks are not subject to the full reporting requirements of Nasdaq, and have sometimes proved dubious.

Once you have researched the stocks that you propose to buy, and found out what index they are on, you need to apply effective buying and selling techniques. We will take a look at how you can do this in the next few paragraphs.

Buying and selling techniques

Buy in small quantities

Users of the Online Share Buyer's FlexiSystem never let penny shares occupy more than 10–15 per cent of their portfolio. This is for two reasons. First, penny shares are speculative, and you should invest only money that you can afford to lose. Second, penny shares have very large spreads, sometimes 25 per cent or higher, which increases the investment risk.

If this is not bad enough, the market makers may only deal in very small amounts at the price specified. The more you try to buy or sell a given penny stock, the more the price will be ratcheted up or down against you.

To increase your chances of making money from penny shares, spread your risk by investing in several companies. Do not try to sell too soon. If you want to sell shares in a relatively illiquid stock, a buyer must be found and this can take time.

Apply trading rules to short-term situations

If you buy penny shares on the basis of market perception, you are entering a short-term trading situation, and some of the rules covered on Day 4 apply. The trick is to catch a penny share early, and ride the rise in share price.

ARM Holdings and Baltimore Technologies are stocks that have seen extreme volatility in the last few years, dropping back substantially from their highs. However, investors who had bought them when they were penny shares have done very well.

A stop loss for penny shares

When you buy penny shares, use a trailing stop loss. Because penny shares can fluctuate so violently, set this at a fairly wide level, perhaps 25 per cent, to make it less likely that you will be selling out on temporary dips.

Market manipulations

Unscrupulous dealers

Unscrupulous dealers often manipulate the penny share market. I am not going to offer names, as some of these firms are very fast to take legal action, and have very deep pockets. Some of these operators appear above board whereas in fact they use various tricks to lure you into investing as much as possible in their dubious share offerings. For more about their wicked techniques, see Day 11.

The conclusion is simple. If you want to buy and sell penny shares, my strong advice to you is to use a *bona fide* member of the London Stock Exchange, and not from a penny share dealer that lacks this credential. Even then, do not buy a penny share only as a result of a share pitch, but conduct your own research.

Next, we will turn our attention to the tax advantages derived from investing in *unquoted* small companies, which includes those on the OFEX and AIM.

Tax advantages

The tax perks available for investing in some unquoted companies are most welcome, although you should never invest only for that reason. In the next few sections, I will explain the main options.

The Enterprise Investment Scheme

The Enterprise Investment Scheme (EIS) was introduced in the November 1993 budget as a not dissimilar replacement for the Business Expansion Scheme. Not all investments offering EIS tax relief are successful, so tread carefully.

To qualify as an individual for EIS tax relief, you must be unconnected with the company in which you plan to invest. This means that you cannot be from the outset an employee, a paid director, or a more-than-30 per cent stakeholder. If you qualify, you may buy shares in a qualifying company, but cannot redeem them for three years.

A qualifying company must be UK-based, unquoted and carrying on a qualifying business, or intending to do so. Companies involved in certain activities are barred from qualifying. These include finance and leasing, law and accountancy, market gardening and farming, forestry and timber, nursing and residential care homes, and hotels.

Income tax relief

You can claim 20 per cent income tax relief on an EIS investment of up to £150,000 in any tax year, and your spouse can claim the same. You will receive the relief in the tax year when you buy the shares, and there are also limited carry-back provisions. Your minimum subscription is normally £500.

Capital gains tax (CGT) relief

If you sell shares subject to EIS income tax relief – that you have held for at least five years – there will be no capital gains tax (CGT) charge on any profits.

In addition, you may defer any amount of CGT on the disposal of assets if you match this with a new subscription for EIS shares. You must do this between a year before, and three years after, the disposal.

The deferred gain is chargeable if you *sell* the new shares, except to a spouse. However, you can continue to defer the tax liability by reinvesting in more EIS schemes.

Venture capital trusts (VCTs)

A venture capital trust (VCT) is a quoted company that holds at least 70 per cent of its investments in qualifying, unquoted companies trading in the UK. No single holding may account for more than 15 per cent of the total.

When you subscribe for new shares in a VCT, you can claim income tax relief at 10 per cent on up to £100,000 per year. If you sell any shares within three years, you will lose this income tax relief proportionately.

However, you can make capital gains of up to £100,000 a year free of CGT, nothwithstanding for how long you have held the shares. In addition, you can defer CGT on other gains for as long as you have reinvested them in a VCT.

Inheritance tax

Once you have held unquoted shares for two years, they are exempt from inheritance tax. This is currently charged at 40 per cent on the net value of an estate after an exemption of £234,000.

Further investigations

The above sections are simply an introduction to a complicated subject. If you are interested in investing in unquoted companies, you will need to assess the tax relief implications in much more detail.

You will find some helpful and up-to-date explanations of the EIS, VCTs, and related tax relief issues at the Web site of the Inland Revenue (www.inlandrevenue.gov.uk). Also visit the Web sites of accountancy firms specializing in tax for investments. Among those that have impressed me are Deloitte & Touche (www.deloitte.co.uk) and Blythens (www.blythens.co.uk). For details of current tax rates, go to www.glazers.co.uk.

General Internet resources

You have now covered a comprehensive programme for selecting and investing in penny shares. Never forget that this is one of the most dangerous areas of investing.

The Internet can be of great help to you but, unless you really know what you are doing, do not act on penny stock tips given online. Use the resource only as a source of education and general ideas.

Based on this proviso, here are some Web sites, often based in the United States, that I have found interesting. Go to Rollercoaster Stocks (www.rollercoasterstocks.com), which has some helpful advice on penny shares generally. Another interesting site is Penny Investor.com (www.pennyinvestor.com) whose founder claims that he has lost US $57,000 from being misled by hype and con-artists in the penny share game, but has now learnt from his mistakes and become a successful trader.

For perspectives on US penny shares and related frauds (also with international application) consult Penny Stock Portal at Ameritech (www.ameritech.net). Read the informative advice from the Office of the Secretary of the State of Missouri (http:mosl.sos.state.mo.us/sos-sec/pens+k.html). On high-risk US pink sheets stocks, go to www.penny-stocks.net.

You may wish to browse through some of the various online tip sheets. These include Penny Shares Ltd.com (www.pennysharesltd.com) which uses technical and fundamental analysis, and has a free e-mail service for updates, and a facility for submitting your stock for analysis. For general advice, see online tipsheet Pennystock insider.com (www.pennystockinsider.com).

In the UK, visit the UK Motley Fool (www.fool.co.uk) where you will find the case against penny shares well represented. On February 19, 2001, this site warned of penny shares: 'The risk of picking the rotten apples far outweigh the rewards of picking the rare good ones'.

The best known UK dealer in penny shares is City Equities. It provides some background information at its Web site (www.cityequities.com). For information on the market-leading newsletter *Red Hot Penny Shares*, visit the Web site of its publisher Fleet Street Publications (www.fleetstreetpublications.co.uk). The best UK books on penny share investing are written, and now self-published by journalist Michael Walters. These are *How to Make A Killing in Penny Shares* and *The £1,000 Share Punter*. For details, visit the author's Web site at www.michaelwalters.com.

For online information on small technology stocks, visit the message boards, features and newslinks at Silicon Investor (www.techstocks.com). Read the informed perspectives of Richard Holway Ltd at its Web site on www.holway.com. For further useful Web sites, see Day 3 and the Appendix.

The way forward

Penny shares are for experts and for mugs, a share dealer who makes his living from this game has claimed. There is a strong element of truth in this. The ones who profit most from penny shares are the specialist traders in the business.

If you want to get involved in penny shares, never buy just on somebody else's tip but conduct your own research. If this last sentence is all you take from this book, it could save you thousands, even tens of thousands of pounds. It could also make you as much, but, sadly, less often.

Dynamic rules of the Online Share Buyer's FlexiSystem

- Recovery stocks can become takeover targets. If you invest in these early enough, you can make significant money.
- Many mining and resource stocks are worthless.
- When there is a housing boom, invest in house-builders and other companies that will reap the rewards.
- When Internet stocks are out of favour, it is an excellent time to buy them.
- Biotech stocks are particularly high risk as fewer than 10 per cent of their products reach clinical development.
- Make your own penny stock selections and do not rely on the help of others.
- Invest in sectors that are popular, but avoid blatantly over-puffed shares.
- Look for leadership as well as technological expertise in the management of Internet and biotechnology companies.
- Seek penny stocks that have strong asset backing.
- Be wary when an item that would normally be an expense in the profit and loss account is made an asset on the balance sheet.
- Be wary if a software company records sales in its accounts before the customers are due to pay.
- Be cautious about investing in OFEX stocks. If you do invest, go for large companies, and research them properly.
- Do not invest much on the basis of sector, or market conditions.
- If you want to buy penny shares in the United States, make sure that the stocks are fully listed.
- Buy penny shares in small quantities and spread your risk.
- When you deal in penny shares, use a stop loss set at a fairly wide level.

- For dealing in penny shares, use a *bona fide* member of the London Stock Exchange.
- Never invest in unquoted companies only for the tax perk.

Day 7
How to make a killing on new issues

Overview

In this module, we will look at new equity issues, and how you can profit from them. We will look at how they are priced, and the process of bringing them to the market, including the issue of timing. We will explore where companies are listed, and how you should apply for new issues.

In addition, I will show you proven ways to research new issues, including use of appropriate Web sites. We will put the role of venture capitalists under scrutiny. As a strategy, we will see why it is often best to flip a new issue, ie buy and sell it quickly, or else to buy only when it has started trading in the secondary market. Finally, we will look at an interesting case study.

How a new issue works

A new issue of shares takes place when a company is floated on the stock market. Subsequently, the company's shares are traded on what is known as the secondary market.

How new issues are priced

Even if you are investing in a *good* company at flotation, it is not enough in itself. The price must be right, and it will be extremely hard for you to assess this.

A new issue of shares is priced according to demand. In a bull market where institutional investors are competing for shares in every hot new issue almost regardless of its quality, the price set can be much higher than the company's fundamental value. Conversely, in a bear market the price can be lower, which could prove a bargain on a medium- to long-term hold.

Who sets the price

The bank or broker organizing the entire deal – known as global coordinator and bookrunner – sets the price. It manages distribution. This is a sought-after job for which the fees are often high. Banks pitch for this role when a company holds a so-called beauty parade as a preliminary to coming to the market.

The bank that wins the job may have expertise in the company's sector, or a special relationship with its country of origin, although these can also create an off-putting perceived conflict of interests. The level of fees charged may matter. In a large new issue of shares, two banks are often appointed as joint global coordinators and joint bookrunners.

The global coordinator appoints a syndicate of banks to help place stock with institutions and private clients, and announces an overall fee structure. In the syndicate there may be one local bank that typically handles private clients (known as retail). The other banks will probably sell mainly to institutions, but there is no fixed rule. Every bank in the syndicate is given a prestigious title such as co-lead manager or co-manager.

Next comes the pre-marketing phase of the deal, which involves meetings between the banks and institutional investors. Based on investor demand, the global coordinator will set a price range representing the proposed perimeters within which the new issue will later be priced. The bank will often, but not always, made this range public.

Knowing the price range is helpful but not enough

Once they know the price range, analysts can put forward a value on the company to be listed, as if priced at the lower, mid and upper end of the range respectively. The valuation will typically be based on the prospective PE ratio or enterprise value/EBITDA ratio (see Day 3) against comparable companies.

Financial journalists, particularly on the *Financial Times* Lex column, or on Web sites providing critical analysis – such as breakingviews.com (to subscribe, contact the site at newsubscriptions @breakingnews.com, telephone: +44 (0)20 7377 2425); or Citywire.co.uk (www.citywire.co.uk) – may report these valuations and provide critical comment.

Such broadbrush perspectives are useful, but until the deal is actually priced, you cannot be confident of projected valuations. Apart from the frequent unreliability of, for instance, prospective earnings figures, this is for the following three reasons:

- The range might be very wide. If the deal is priced at the bottom of the range, this could make a very substantial difference to the valuation compared with having the deal priced at the top. A prospective valuation based on a mid-range price is perhaps not specific enough.
- Banks involved in the flotation may move the price range up or down to meet changing demand levels. This shifting of the goalposts happens only occasionally, but enough not to be dismissed as a possibility. If the price range is increased, the deal is likely to be priced at the top of the range.
- The deal may be postponed indefinitely. In such a case, the brokers involved will often announce that they will refloat the company pending better market conditions.

The postponement may happen after the market has slid severely between when the range was set and the deal was priced. In the year following April 2000, many deals in major markets were pulled due to poor market conditions

When deals are postponed, part of the problem is often that an immature company is involved. Tell-tale symptoms include the company making a loss, with no firm prospects of breaking into profit, and having limited revenues. Only in a bull market will investors possibly disregard such factors. Sometimes, a postponed deal may never come to the market again.

The demand creation game

In establishing demand for a new issue, the price range, and subsequent price, are crucial. If the bookrunner prices an issue low enough, this will spur over-subscription. To some extent, this concept is a technicality as institutional investors that want stock will always apply for more than they expect to receive.

In a bull market, a subtle way to create demand for new equity issuance is through controlled release of news to the media. This is the task of the PR agencies working for flotation candidates. It is a delicate art that can backfire, particularly in the long run, as some journalists like to assert their independence.

On the road

Following the pre-marketing of a deal and the setting of its price range, the bookbuilding process takes place. In this phase, the banks build up the book of demand for the new issue. At road show, they present the company to institutional investors, either in groups or, more effectively, in individual meetings dubbed one-to-ones.

Secrets of the bookbuild period

Bookbuilding is a tense period for the banks handling the pending new issue in which you will find it difficult to find out how institutions are reacting. Institutional interest that was established at the pre-marketing phase can easily wane on adverse market conditions or other news.

Institutions tend to hold off their orders for shares until only shortly before the end of the bookbuild period, which will typically last two or three weeks. The investment banks involved put up with all this uncertainty because new issues represent some of their most lucrative business.

New issues need private clients

Syndicate bankers welcome your involvement in new issues for less-than-altruistic reasons. Retail investors (private clients) can swell out the order book. Most lack the analytical skills, corporate data, and contacts to value a company effectively. The Internet is narrowing the financial information access gap between private and institutional investors, but it has not yet closed it. With retail investors involved, banks can price a new issue higher than otherwise.

Unsurprisingly, retail involvement in new equity issues is on the increase. At this transitional stage, private investors are well represented in some new issues, but not in others.

How to select and apply for new issues

Where companies are listing

If you want to play as safe as possible, invest in companies that are being floated only on the London Stock Exchange. The AIM has greater share price volatility as it is less stringently regulated. Avoid new issues of companies on OFEX unless you have specialist knowledge or are a gambler. For more about these last two junior markets, see Day 6.

Some stocks may be listed abroad, or in more than one country simultaneously. In Western Europe, most new high-tech markets such as Germany's Neuer Markt and Italy's Nuovo Mercato had proved resilient in their formative phases, but later succumbed to adverse global market conditions.

In the United States, Nasdaq, the high-tech market, is highly volatile. It has some spectacular successes, but all too many small high-tech stocks that have floated on Nasdaq over the last three years have joined its so-called graveyard of poor performers.

How to apply for new issues

If you want to invest in a new issue in the UK or abroad, you can often apply through your online (or advisory) broker. Alternatively, use a Web site that specializes in new issues. For Internet company flotations, you must sometimes apply directly to the floating company through its Web site.

When you apply for a new issue online, you will download a form, which you must complete and send with your cheque to the global coordinator of the deal by (excuse the term) snail mail. Be careful to fill in the form correctly. Do not make multiple applications as these are easily discovered and can lead to prosecution.

In these ways, and through the provision of relevant information and research online, the Internet is making new issues available to a wider investor base. Be wary. It is all too easy to be seduced by glowing online write-ups of flotation candidates, and technology that enables the application process seem no more complicated than pressing a few keys on your computer. But, the deal may not be that good, and the subscription process may not work.

In March 2000, my colleagues and I tried to register for the share offering of a Scandinavian Internet company. The procedure was fraught with technical hitches, and the prospectus not easily downloadable. Others found the same problem, according to message boards on financial Web sites.

In new equity issues generally, private investors will typically receive a limited allocation of shares in proportion to their demand. The financial institutions running the deal give priority of allocation to their large institutional clients. This can also serve as a safeguard for private clients.

In retrospect it was a relief to those who subscribed in early 2000 to the new issue of lastminute.com, the Internet leisure services company, that only 35 shares per person were allocated. For more details of this unfortunate flotation, turn to the end of this module.

Research new issues before you invest

Before you decide whether to invest in a new issue, research the company as thoroughly as possible.

The syndicate desk

If you ring the syndicate desk of the global coordinator to a new issue, you may find a friendly person who will discuss the deal, but don't rely on it. The bankers are not obliged to help you, and are more interested in institutional investors.

If a banker does speak to you about the new issue, read between the lines. To say that bankers lie through their teeth during bookbuilding is not quite fair as, in the face of immense commercial pressure, they are usually scrupulous in their choice of words. Let us merely say that they definitely put the best gloss on the deal and will not admit problems. I have known bankers wax lyrical about a bookbuild, and how major institutions have already placed big orders – then, hours later, the deal is pulled due to lack of demand.

The analysts

If you approach the relevant sector analyst working for the bank that is handling the deal, the analyst may give you his or her research (see Day 3 on how to persuade him or her). If so, be cautious about trusting its conclusions. As a result of the corporate link, this analyst will probably have a superior grasp of the company's business, but will also be biased.

As a result, the analyst's discounted cash flow analysis may value the company at a level that the bank's corporate finance division will have discreetly dictated. One leading syndicate banker confided in me that, in bull markets, he and his colleagues dictate what the analysts write.

Also, listen to the views of analysts in leading City banks that are uninvolved in the deal. Again, be sceptical. The analysts do not always put what they think in their written reports for fear of offending companies. Also, they are often wrong.

Financial journalists are less knowledgeable than analysts, but are also less inhibited. They are not hindered by the so-called blackout period which prevents those directly involved with a new equity issue from releasing information about it in advance. They are not so hampered with conflicts of interests.

On a personal level, some journalists are resentful of the industry that they write about and are only too keen to put the boot in. They can get information leaks from banks anxious to scupper the business of their rivals, or from disgruntled employees. Partly for such reasons, reporting even in highly regarded newspapers and trade magazines is not always reliable or complete.

Despite this, financial journalists have access to expertise and their ear to the ground. If they collectively agree that a deal is over- or under-priced, they will very likely be right.

Some useful Internet sites and publications

For independent journalistic comment on new issues, browse some of the major financial Web sites for private clients, particularly the Motley Fool UK (www.motleyfool.co.uk) and Citywire (www.citywire.co.uk).

You will not find such detached comment on the Web sites of those companies that were established to promote new issues via the Internet. This is understandable as they are directly involved in the sales process. Their sites may, however, give you useful facts about the deal, including how much money is being raised, the banks involved, what the company does, how long it has been operating, and details of the management. You may find related interviews here, and a prospectus for downloading.

If the new issues bug bits hard, you may wish to tackle the news sources of the professionals. Try *Financial News*, a gossipy weekly magazine aimed primarily at bankers. For the online version, visit www.efinancialnews.com, where you may register for regular e-mails of news updates.

Another useful source, if you can afford it, is *International Financing Review*, a subscription-only magazine published by Thomson Financial, which also has a Web site (www.ifrweb.com). I declare an interest as I write extensively for this publication.

The grey market

Another way to keep abreast of sentiment about a pending new issue is to check its grey market price. This refers to the value that the spread betting firms put on the shares before the deal is priced.

Be warned. Grey market prices are an unreliable predictor. In some share issues, the grey market price has been high, but the stock has plummeted far below these valuation levels shortly after flotation.

Do not overrate the involvement of leading banks or venture capitalists

If leading investment banks are involved in a new issue, do not be automatically reassured. This is no guarantee that the flotation candidate is a good company, or that it is being offered at a good price. The banks earn usually substantial fees from handling the flotation, regardless of how well the shares do in the secondary market.

If major venture capitalists (VCs) are backing a flotation candidate, again do not assume that this will benefit you as an investor. In practice, a flotation will often have been planned from the start to provide the VC with an exit from its investment early at a handsome profit. You may not have the same opportunity.

Nonetheless, keep an eye on the VCs. By their early involvement, they have enormous influence on the capital markets. They select many of the companies that will ultimately be floated – or that will find a strategic buyer – and the investment banks follow their lead. Also watch the Internet incubator funds, which offer preliminary support for some companies before they seek VC backing.

Timing of the flotation

The timing of a flotation typically depends on market conditions, which are notoriously fickle. The weaker the market, the more of a solid track record a flotation candidate needs to interest institutional investors. In July 2000, against the backdrop of a volatile stock market, Robert Walters, the recruitment agency, floated on the London Stock Exchange and saw its shares soar above issue price. The company had excellent management, and a good profit record, and these proved the secrets of the deal's success.

In the case of outstanding high-tech companies coming to the market, a track record is not essential. Also in July 2000, Orchestream was an unprofitable young high-tech company that floated on the London Stock Exchange and saw its shares soar well above issue price in early secondary market trading. The reason was that its business model was exceptionally strong, according to bankers close to the deal.

When market conditions deteriorated further in 2001, some young high-tech companies with a similarly strong business model postponed a planned flotation. At such times, there is no substitute for an established business rooted in the old economy, with strong revenues, and profits either ongoing or expected in the foreseeable future.

Favoured sectors

If you are going to buy and sell quickly, it makes sense to go for favoured sectors. Otherwise, be more cautious.

Be wary of some investment trusts. They may offer free warrants as a sweetener to the new issue. But, to compensate, the bookrunner may price the stock at a premium to net asset value. As a result, the stock may fall to below net asset value in early secondary market trading. Furthermore, if you are issued with only a few warrants, it may not be worthwhile selling them in the market as the commission payable could wipe out any profits.

Upon issue

Get flipping mad

Once you have bought into a new issue, it is often best to flip or stag the shares, ie to sell them quickly, as soon as secondary market trading starts. This is particularly so if the share price is higher than the stock's fundamental value. Many institutional investors flip new issues.

Unsurprisingly, the financial institutions that organized the flotation will try to discourage flipping of the stock. This is because a mass exodus from a new issue could send the share price into free fall, making the deal appear to have been overpriced. In its turn, this can bring adverse publicity, and the bank may be forced to support the price in various ways.

In trying to keep clients in the stock, the banks involved will typically focus their most vigorous attentions on you, the private client. They will not dare to criticize the major institutional investors that flip the stock as they need their participation in future share offerings. If, therefore, the banks advises a buy-and-hold strategy, do not necessarily cooperate. A buy-and-hold strategy works only if you bought for value in the first place and, with new issues, this is not always the case.

In July 2000, the flotation of mobile telephone retailer Carphone Warehouse set a new level of pressure on private clients not to flip new issues. In this deal, run by investment bank Credit Suisse First Boston, private investors, unlike institutions, received priority allocation only if they committed themselves to holding the shares for three months. Some market commentators expressed outrage at what they felt was discrimination against the private client.

Sometimes the company itself takes the initiative in attracting and retaining private investors. We saw earlier in this module how, as a condition of subscribing to the new issue of shares in an Internet company, you may be required to register with its Web site. The company may then swamp you with e-mails promoting and trying to sell its services or trying to get you to visit its site. This can be very tiresome.

The Internet companies that bombard registered subscribers with e-mails do not always offer a workable procedure for deregistering. On a number of occasions, I attempted to unsubscribe to one recently floated Internet company's e-mailing list without success. I then telephoned the company, having found its telephone number on the Web site, and asked to unsubscribe. I was assured that it had been done. Again, no luck. I had to ring and complain twice more before my name was removed.

Buy recently issued stock in the secondary market

If a new issue was overpriced, or if it took place in adverse market conditions, you may do well to wait until the share price has fallen in secondary market trading *before* you buy.

Let me give you an example. I know of investors who bought into the mobile telephone company Orange at around E~8.50 per share shortly after the company was floated in February 2001 at E~10. By April, the share price had risen to E~11.1, and these buyers in the secondary market, unlike the original subscribers, were seeing a small profit on their investment.

Case study

A high-profile overpriced deal

Let us look at an example of an overpriced deal. The Internet leisure services provider, lastminute.com, was floated on the London Stock Exchange in March 2000.

At this point, investors had a blind, almost evangelical belief that all companies in the Internet sector had an excellent and fast-track future. Investors and banking professionals fanned the flames, giving high valuations to Internet companies that lacked any sort of track record.

Valuations of such companies (see Day 3) often focused on the business model, and lastminute.com, despite limited revenues and a lack of profitability, had a clever one. It operated as a middleman between retailers such as airlines offloading cheap tickets and consumers. The company advertised its services on London buses and its technology was state-of-the-art.

A hot company

When lastminute.com came to the market, investors were excited. Here was the chance to grab a piece of a really hot company. US bank Morgan Stanley Dean Witter as global coordinator to the deal raised the price range by 67 per cent shortly before flotation due to the heavy demand. The new issue was priced at 380p per share, which was at the top of the revised range.

In early secondary market trading, lastminute.com saw its shares plummet in value as the broader high-tech market corrected itself. By September, the company was trading at 146p, which was well under half flotation level. It later fell to less than half this reduced level. Many syndicate bankers criticized how the lastminute.com flotation had been handled. 'The deal was overpriced with no leeway,' one said.

A stock to flip

Lastminute.com had been a stock to flip. Investors who had sold out early could have made a good profit. Many had been unable to do this as they had not received their share certificates in time. I had been in that position, and had found that the company was unwilling to address its administrative inefficiencies. In my efforts to obtain my share certificates, I had rung a supposed helpline and been passed from one unhelpful person or answerphone to another.

In April 2000, I documented the whole sorry experience on the leader pages of *The Daily Telegraph* where I concluded that the private investor was at a considerable disadvantage to his or her professional counterpart.

The way forward

Largely thanks to the Internet, new issues are becoming much more accessible to private investors. Here is an opportunity, but select the new issues in which you invest carefully. In bull markets particularly, plenty of dud companies come to the market, and the price of shares issued may bear no relation to their value.

Dynamic rules of the Online Share Buyer's FlexiSystem

- Research a new equity issue thoroughly before you invest your money. Do not trust analysts working for the banks handling the flotation.
- Shares at issue may have a price unrelated to their fundamental value.
- It is often best to flip newly issued shares, ie to buy and sell them quickly.
- If you are buying into a new issue for the long term, try to make sure that the company is cheap on fundamentals.
- If the issue price seems too high, put off your buying decision until the stock is trading in the secondary market.
- To play safe, go for new issues on the London Stock Exchange rather than the junior markets or abroad.
- Check the grey market price of a pending new issue as an indicator of demand, but do not rely on this.
- Do not assume that a new issue will make you money only because it is backed by top-name banks and/or venture capitalists.
- Avoid new issues of investment trusts that are overpriced to compensate for free warrants offered.

Day 8
Secrets of stock tipsters

Overview

In this module, we will look at the influential but flawed share tipping business. I will show you what kind of people the tipsters are, how they select stocks, and how they attract a following.

Armed with this knowledge, you will be better able to discriminate between the various tip sheets on the market. I will show you how to assess a tip sheet's track record, and we will look at what kind of companies are covered best.

We will see how valuable the Internet can be, not just for gaining access to star tipsters, but also for assessing them. Finally, we will take an inside look at the exciting but corrupt world of Internet message boards.

The share tipping game

The background of share tipsters

Stock market tipsters are an opportunistic bunch. Some work for newspapers, but most for specialist subscription-only newsletters. These are increasingly being offered and/or published via the Internet.

The tipsters have an influence that may or may not be proportional to their track record. Some tip sheets have hit and surpassed the 30,000 subscription level, while others – even long-established newsletters with a high profile – have been hard-pressed to get anywhere near that.

Share tipsters, even when highly acclaimed, are usually far from being financial geniuses. Many have little understanding of finance. They do not have the skill to dissect the latest company report and accounts, even though they may refer to this primary source in their articles.

Their usual background is financial journalism, which requires the ability to summarize complex arguments, but not much more. It does not require financial acumen or any serious level of numeracy. Some will have once worked in the City of London or on Wall Street, but this does not in itself add value to their investment advice. The old adage applies, if they know so much about picking stocks, why are they not investing their own money for a living?

Many tipsters are too lazy, under-resourced or time-stretched to develop contacts in the City and among companies. For some, writing for or editing tip sheets is not their full-time job. In researching tips, many take the easy option, which is to use secondary sources. The game works as follows. The tipster lifts stories from newspapers, other tip sheets, and the message boards on his or her financial Web sites – the very places to which you yourself have access. The tipster will then represent these stories with a different emphasis, or a new fact, passing them off as his or her own work. In this way, the tipster will present recommendations – even if largely lifted from an obscure Web site – in a seamless and professional way, with an air of authority.

The secret of successful tipping is to write convincingly, perhaps entertainingly. It is not based on how many recommendations turn out well.

As a crucial part of his or her presentation, the tipster will often hint at City contacts and confidential tip-offs. Alternatively, tipsters may represent themselves as advocates for the 'person in the street', sifting through the muddle that emanates from the City, and coming out with solid recommendations. One highly successful tip sheet editor boasts that he writes his tip sheet in the language that people speak in his local pub.

If a tipster wants to keep his or her reputation intact, it can pay not to be associated with one Web site or newsletter for too long, as its tipping record will at some point go through a lean period. For this reason, newsletter editors and writers are often willing to move jobs. Many tipsters operate anonymously. Some have been known to develop a non-existent 'contact' to whom they may give a posh-sounding name. This *alter ego* appears real to their subscribers, as if of a City gent with all the right connections.

As an alternative strategy, ambitious tip sheet writers try to develop a high profile name. They try to build up a following by infusing their personality into their writing. Tipsters are at their most convincing – and their most suspect – when they hold shares in the company themselves, which is sometimes the case. Their newsletters may or may not declare this interest in the small print. Other tipsters have never invested directly in shares in their lives.

The track record

The tipster will typically claim a sound track record for forecasting share tips or market movements. To substantiate this, he or she may cite the successful tips and gloss over the failures. Tipsters are under no legal obligation to tell the full story. The successes may be temporary. When a tip is given prominence in a popular newsletter, the market makers increase the price. Other tipsters get wind and steal the idea. It is a vicious circle which can send up the share price temporarily, and then back down again.

Some tip sheets promise to return your subscription fee if at least several of their tips have not doubled in the year. They may make so many tips that the forfeit never arises. Although the tip sheets can sometimes point you in the direction of interesting companies, they are an adjunct and not a substitute for your own research.

Be particularly wary about following share tips in the newspapers. The journalists will often have received their tips from a PR consultant pushing the company. They are doing him or her a favour in return for pushing more stories their way. They do not really know about the value of their tip, and do not care.

Take a trial newsletter subscription

Most online and other newsletters offer trial subscriptions or free copies. Always take advantage of this, and see how a newsletter's tips turn out before you commit your money on its advice.

For free samples of financial newsletters, visit one of the Web sites that specialize in this service. At the time of writing, two such sites that I sometimes visit are at www.financial-freebies.com, and at www.thefreestuffgallery.com.

Specialist tip sheet coverage

Penny shares

The most popular tip sheets focus on penny shares. This is mainly because investors love them, but also because independent advice in this area is not otherwise easily available. For more about penny shares, see Day 6.

Growth companies

Many newsletters focus more broadly on growth companies. Their success rate often tracks market conditions, looking good in bull markets but less so in a market downturn.

The most prominent of these tip sheets available on the Web at the time of writing is Tom Winnifrith's t1ps.com (www.t1ps.com). Winnifrith is a former investment analyst who was founding editor of *Red Hot Penny Shares*, a successful penny share newsletter published by the Fleet Street Letter Group. Winnifrith is a talented journalist who thoroughly researches the companies he writes about. His Web site has innovative features, including audio interviews with big players in the penny stock business, and an e-mail alert service. Like many tip sheet writers, he has a variable track record.

Value investing

In my view, the best newsletters focus on value investing. They make mistakes but do not pander to popular opinion. The writers will apply a series of value filters in selecting stocks. They may look for undervalued growth stocks, or for mature companies that have fallen out of favour and so trade at bargain prices.

One prominent player is Hemmington Scott. It runs an online tipping service which, at the time of writing, is available on a free month's trial (www.hemscott.net). From this stable comes the newsletter *Investing for Growth*, which was devised and initially edited by UK investment guru Jim Slater (see Day 3 and Day 12).

The newsletter applies Slater's value filters, and has enjoyed spectacular successes, but also some failures.

On the basis of track record and depth of comment, probably the best investment newsletter in the field of value investing, and in the UK market generally, is *analyst*. The writers, who are *bona fide* analysts and not journalists, are heavily influenced by the stock-tipping principles of pioneering US value investor Warren Buffett. The publication sometimes makes mistakes, particularly on timing. But its recommendations are based on a proven, workable system that requires a thorough understanding of the company.

If you are a subscriber to *analyst*, you will have access also to the publication's Web site (www.analystinvestor.com). This contains all past company research in an archive that you can access online. It offers useful articles on investment techniques, and message boards.

I recommend that you attend *analyst* day seminars run in Central London. In early 2001, I attended the *Sage of Omaha* day-long course – so named after Warren Buffett. The course, attended particularly by self-employed business people, focused on value investing techniques in detail. It was a more intelligent seminar than most aimed at private investors, and more impartial in its approach.

Contrarian investment

Contrarian investing is unpopular in a bull market, to the likely detriment of its newsletters that specialize in this area. In June 2000, The Hirsch Organization, based in New Jersey, discontinued publication of its *Beating the Dow* newsletter, which had focused on investing in high-dividend blue-chip stocks. It admitted that the newsletter's portfolio had not achieved an outstanding performance at a time when high-tech stocks were in vogue. Subscription levels had fallen below breakeven level.

Alternative international investing

Typically, the high-profile newsletter editors turn themselves into the stuff of legends with cunning self-publicity campaigns across continents. Many have tried to emulate investment newsletter editor Chevalier Harry D (for Dynamic) Schultz, KHC, KM, KCPR, KCSA, KCSS, and few have succeeded.

I met Schultz – whom the *Guinness Book of Records* has in the past categorized as one of the world's most highly paid investment advisers – when he was about 70 years old, and going strong, at an investment conference in Monte Carlo 10 years before the millennium. The guru was grateful when a friend of mine offered to recommend him for fellowship of the Royal Society of Arts, which would enable him to add FRSA to the letters already after his name.

The Schultz newsletter business boasts devoted subscribers. The International Harry Schultz Letter has sometimes been written in an abbreviated prose (U instead of you, for example). It seeks to attract subscribers online (www.hsletter.com). Unfortunately its track record has not always been good. If you had followed its advice over one 12-year period, you would have done significantly less well than the average, according to US-based *The Hulbert Guide to Financial Newsletters.*

Harry Schultz is a pioneer in the world of unconventional tax avoidance techniques. I do not recommend getting involved in this broad area unless you really understand what you are doing. But to find out more for interest's sake, look on the pages of The Sovereign Society (www.sovereignsociety.com). You can gain access also from the Web site of Eden Press, a California-based alternative tax haven information bookseller (www.edenpress.com). The Sovereign Society offers a fascinating free e-newsletter which focuses on offshore tax havens, tax avoidance, and related matters from an international perspective.

Investment gurus on the Web

Generally, before you follow an investment guru's advice, check his or her track record. For instance, based on his track record, I always pay attention to what Peter Temple writes on the Ample Web site (www.ample.com). He has worked as an investment analyst and has a strong understanding of the stock market, including from the online perspective.

I am more wary of the stock recommendations of Michael Walters that, at the time of writing, I receive via a regular e-mail. Walters is sincere, and applies common sense to his tips. He has the popular touch. All this has doubtless contributed to the significant following he has built up from his past years as deputy City editor on the

Daily Mail. Unfortunately, although he has had his successes, he has also made some mistakes, and his powers of analysis are, like those of most financial journalists, limited.

On the Motley Fool UK Web site (www.fool.co.uk), I can never resist reading a buy or sell case presented engagingly by, among others, self-styled chief UK Fool David Berger, and managing editor Bruce Jackson. But I avoid allowing this to influence my own investment decisions. These Fools, like any stock market gurus, have made some serious mistakes.

Investors' own experience of tipsters

The message boards at leading financial Web sites will often reveal how investors feel about tipsters. For example, in February 1999, Interactive Investor International (now Ample) asked its site visitors: 'Many readers think tipsters such as Tom Winnifrith, Paul Kavanagh and Michael Walters have tipped one too many duds. Do you agree?' A staggering 80.39 per cent of those who voted on this less-than-complimentary proposition agreed, and only 5.94 per cent disagreed. The rest did not know.

Of course, no tipster is infallible. Investors can forgive tipsters for a few buying errors. But if a tipster recommends a full buy-and-hold strategy that results in huge, unnecessary losses as the share price plummets, this will cause resentment. Note this online comment about one tipster:

> The fundamentals are right, he always says of shares he recommends . . . his arrogance kept people hanging in when they [the shares] were falling . . . and so many people trusted him and paid him for what they thought was his competence . . . Be ashamed [tipster] . . . you couldn't even help people get out . . . I've lost a lot of money.

Some pundits are too focused on a pet sector. One investor complained online:

> That twerp. He always overrates technology stocks. He thinks he knows it all. He tipped shares and they went up in a bull market. Big deal. He is dangerous. He'll see the upside on

anything, even a dive bomber ... [Given] the long list of casualties, he no doubt will blame the market, but his tips are supposed to outperform it.

More about Internet message boards

Useful as they are, the Internet message boards are unreliable. Some contributors are sincere, although their quality of input will vary. Others will recommend or denigrate a stock for dishonourable purposes. They may aim to influence buying of the stock so that they can buy or sell at a more congenial price on their own account. Alternatively, they may be the stooges of professional stock manipulators. When you visit the message boards for research purposes, *caveat emptor* prevails.

It is particularly difficult to detect those who are criticizing stocks in order to send the share price down. Under several aliases, these operators will refer repeatedly in their posts to news that adversely affects the company, and has at least some truth. By criticizing a stock little and often, they cast doubt on it. They set themselves up as experts, and berate their victim companies for falling short of impossibly high standards.

These insincere stock critics also tell untruths, but cunningly, on matters where you are unable or unlikely to check, on which the company itself has shown reticence. Investors who sell a stock too early and lose out may join them.

When you use the Internet message boards, you will come across such regular manipulators. Some are more obvious than others. Do not argue or reason with them. You would be not only wasting your time, but would give them the attention that they crave. Instead attend to messages from those who post only occasionally but seem to have something to say. If you are interested in the underlying stock, check any matters raised with the company itself or another reliable source.

The way forward

The key point that you should take away from this module is that you cannot rely on someone else's share tip. As I have stressed throughout this book, the onus is on you to become self reliant, and make your own investment decisions.

Dynamic rules of the Online Share Buyer's FlexiSystem

- Do not follow tipsters blindly, but use them as an indicator of potentially interesting companies.
- Be particularly wary of share tips in newspapers. PR consultants pushing the companies are likely to have generated these.
- Growth company tip sheets do well in bull markets, but not so well when conditions turn bearish.
- The best newsletters are orientated towards value investing. They make mistakes but do not pander to popular opinion.
- To find out how investors feel about individual tipsters, read the message boards at leading financial Web sites.
- Before you follow an investment guru's advice, check his or her track record.
- Do not argue or reason with those who seek to manipulate the message boards.
- If you come across a potentially important point on the message boards, check it with the underlying company or with another reliable source.

Day 9
How to profit from traded options and warrants

Overview

In this module, you will find enough information about traded options and warrants to get you started in this specialized form of investment. First, we will define traded options and look at how they can be used for speculation and hedging.

You will find here the most popular relevant for trading strategies explained, whether as a buyer of options or, on the other side of the fence, as a writer. We will touch upon advanced trading positions, including the butterfly and the tarantula.

You will learn how to become your own options analyst, and to avoid the worst trading risks. I have listed some useful online research sources for you, and identified suitable brokers.

This module also explains warrants, and how they work. The practicalities of dealing in these are covered.

How options work

What is an option?

An option is a financial instrument that enables you to bet on the movement of individual shares or indices, as well as of currencies, commodities or interest rates. It gives you the right, but not the obligation, to buy or sell a security at a pre-determined price (strike or exercise price) within a specified time period or (less commonly) at a specified time.

Traditional and traded options

If you have a traditional option, you must exercise it (buy or sell the underlying security) to establish any profit that may be available to you. This form of option is now unpopular because it is not very flexible.

Traded options, which came to the UK in 1978, are the modern preferred alternative, and we are only concerned with these in this module. You can exercise a traded option, or, as most prefer, simply trade it in the market place.

US- and European-style options

If you have an option in the US style (in which traded options are available), you can exercise it at any time between when the option comes to market, and its expiry. This is typically a five-month period, but there are some options with expiry dates set two years ahead.

If you have an option in the less popular European style, you can exercise it only on the expiry date. The third alternative is a capped option. This gives you the right to exercise the option only during a specified period, unless the option reaches the cap value before expiry, in which case the option is automatically exercised on your behalf.

Call and Put options

As a traded options buyer, you must choose between two alternatives. First, a Call option, which gives you the right but not the obligation to *buy* the underlying security at the strike price. Second, a Put option, which gives you as options buyer the right but not the obligation to *sell* the security at the strike price.

As a buyer of a Call or Put option, you are on one side of the fence. The writer of the option is on the other. In the case of a Call option, the writer is obliged to sell the shares at the strike price if the buyer requires it. Conversely, for a Put option, the writer may be obliged to buy the shares at the strike price. In compensation for taking this risk, the writer receives a premium from the buyer. This premium is the market price that you, as an option buyer, will pay for an option. You may pay only part of the premium up front. This reduced amount is known as margin. If your position moves away from profitability, you will have to top up your margin with so-called variation margin.

If you buy an option, you can make money if the price of the underlying share or index moves in the right direction beyond the extent of the premium that the option writer received from you. In contrast, the option writer makes money if the price does not move this far, or goes in the wrong direction for you as buyer. In this case, the option writer will not have to sell or buy shares to meet your demand, and he or she will pocket the premium.

In the money

When you buy a Call option, you will select from a range of strike prices. If the strike price is lower than the underlying security's current market price, the option is *in the money*, with the difference between the strike price and the current market price representing its value. If the strike price is higher than the current market price, the Call option is *out of the money*, and the premium will be relatively low.

When you buy a Put option, you will again select from a range of strike prices. If the strike price is higher than the share price, the option is *in the money*. If the strike price is lower than the option, it is *out of the money*.

Options are *in* and *out of* the money at different times. As an option moves deeper into the money, the premium rises. Conversely, as it moves more out of the money, the option becomes cheaper. When the strike price is equal to the current market price, this is *at the money*.

Intrinsic and time values

Intrinsic value is how far the underlying stock's value surpasses the option strike price. An option, therefore, has intrinsic value only when it is *in the money*.

The option's time value is defined as its total value less intrinsic value. The more time an option has until it expires, the higher this figure will be, as the underlying share price has a correspondingly greater chance of changing in the option buyer's favour.

A highly geared financial instrument

As a traded option buyer, you can trade with small amounts of money and make proportionately much higher gains than if you were investing in the underlying share or index. Conversely, if the option does not go as planned, you will lose your entire investment – in percentage terms enormous but, in actual terms, not necessarily much. On the other side of the fence, the option writer makes frequent profits, but risks potentially unlimited losses.

In these ways, the option is highly geared, rising or falling in value much more dramatically than the underlying security. Traders find the upside potential attractive, and the options market, despite its high risks, has seen around 40 per cent compound annual growth a year since the late 1980s.

Your LIFFE line

In the UK, options trading is run by the London International Financial Futures and Options Exchange, which has an informative Web site (www.liffe.co.uk). At any time, the 100 top UK companies, and some stock market indices, have traded options contracts on LIFFE. The standard contract size is for 1000 shares in a company.

Options on LIFFE have expiry dates grouped three, six or nine months ahead. A first group of companies has the expiry dates of January, April, July and October; a second group has February, May, August and November; while a third expires March, June, September and December. This way, in any given month, options for only about a third of the relevant companies will expire.

Basic strategies

Trade options for profit

In respect of traded options, you can trade options for profit. This is more usual than exercising the traded options, and is sometimes more profitable. But it is a high risk–high reward initiative.

This strategy may appeal if, as an investor, you want big rewards fast, and are prepared to take risks to achieve this. In this case, you will need to have time to watch the market closely. Fortunately, options are a very liquid market, which means that you can usually complete your trades.

Despite the risks, trading options for profit is speculative investing and not gambling. For every buyer of an option there is a seller, but neither side has the odds intrinsically stacked in its favour. There is no casino that rakes in the overwhelming majority of the profits.

Hedge your position

You can also use options to hedge a position that you may have in a share or index. For instance, if you believe the market will crash, you can buy Put options for a company in which you hold shares. This way, if the share price crashes, you can compensate by selling the Puts for a profit. By this hedging technique, you will have protected your position.

Two bullish strategies

If you think the underlying security or index will rise significantly in the short term, buy a Call option. You may foresee such a rise if, for example, the company is the target of a rumoured takeover bid or you are expecting good news.

Remember that you are not obliged to exercise the traded option which, in the case of a Call, would require owning (or acquiring) the underlying shares so that you can sell them in the market to realize your option gain. Instead, you may conveniently sell your traded option on the market and cash in on any profit.

A riskier alternative strategy to buying a Call option is to become the writer of a Put option. This way, you will receive the premium from the buyer, which is the main attraction of the deal. Usually, the Put option sold will expire worthless, and you will keep the premium (10–15 per cent of the gain) without having to buy the underlying stock.

However, if the share price falls below the strike price, your profits will decrease until a point when you start losing money. Your loss will never be more than the value of the underlying share as its value cannot fall below 0 pence.

City professionals do not like writing Put options. I know of one woman who lost a fortune writing Puts during the initial market correction of high-tech stocks in March and April 2000.

Two bearish strategies

If you think that the company's share price will plummet, your simplest strategy is to buy a Put option. However, as an alternative, you could write a Call option. This way, you will take the premium from the buyer, and will keep it if the share price does not rise above the strike price.

If you write a so-called naked Call, this means that you do not own the shares that you are selling. If the share price collapses, you will then have to buy shares at the prevailing market price to keep your part of the deal. To avoid the risks involved in this, you can write covered Calls, which are when you sell Calls on shares that you already own.

If in doubt, straddle

A common options trading strategy is a straddle. Use this as a way to make profits when you expect the underlying stock to move significantly, but you don't know in which direction.

In a so-called long straddle, you will buy a Call option and Put option at an identical strike price and expiration dates. This sounds a wonderful compromise. However, the catch is that the share price has to move up or down a lot – to get past the expense of two premiums rather than the usual one (as well as the high commission costs applicable to a straddle) – if you are to make money.

Advanced strategies

Wheeling and dealing

Professional options traders use other, far more complex techniques. Under a *break forwards*, for instance, the options buyer can break the contract with the writer. Under *participating forwards*, the buyer can benefit from the upside of an option while having some protection from the downside.

Butterflies and condors

If you imagined that bulls and bears were the only animals in the stock market farmyard, think again. Market professionals use various combinations of Puts and Calls to protect their positions while gambling on the future direction of a stock or index. One such strategy is the butterfly, which uses four options, and three strike prices. Alternatively, there is the condor spread, also known as the top hat spread.

Spider power

In a class of its own is the tarantula. This metaphorical spider has eight legs, each representing different futures and options contracts that expire on the same date. If a contract lapses, a leg *breaks* but it can *heal*. If several legs are damaged, the tarantula can become *crippled*, but may recover when markets turn volatile.

Alternatively, a second spider may be introduced with thicker legs that correct the failed legs of its predecessor. In this case, the spiders are said to have *mated*. The spider presence is prominent in the so-called Egyptian ratchet where a contract is repurchased at a lower price to average out a losing position.

Risk warnings

Do not gamble

Options can be bad for your wealth if they lead you to gamble. In unfortunate instances, professionals have done this illicitly and unsuccessfully with other people's money. The story of Nick Leeson who destroyed investment bank Barings by gambling on derivatives is a worst-case example.

Leeson was a 28-year old from Watford who had notoriously failed his maths A-level. Starting out as a settlement clerk at Barings, he was by 1993 a star trader and general manager in the bank's Singapore office. His trading strategies were largely based on arbitrage, which means profiting from often minute price differentials between the same securities on different markets.

The beginning of the end

In January 1995, Barings started writing Put and Call options on the Nikkei 225 index at the same exercise price. This created a straddle from which Barings as options writer would keep the premiums only if the index stayed within the 19,000–21,000 trading range. On January 17, Kobe and Osaka were hit by a huge earthquake and the Nikkei 225 fell below the 19,000 level, putting Barings' profits at risk. On January 23, the index was down to 17,950.

Leeson started buying March and June 95 futures contracts, which were a bet on an improvement in the market. But the Nikkei 225 deteriorated further, and eventually Barings had lost more than £800 million, which was more than its capital. The Bank of England did not bail out Barings as some had expected and, eventually, Dutch insurer ING acquired the bust bank.

Avoid the worst risks

Even on a much smaller scale, options trading is risky. However, as dealers are quick to point out, options reduce your risk as an investor because you will commit less money in absolute terms than you would on the equivalent underlying securities. In addition, you can diversify by taking options on a variety of underlying securities, and by buying both Puts and Calls.

As a general rule, you will find it less risky to buy options than to write them. When you buy, select options on shares or indices that are volatile enough to provide a chance of the big move in your favour that you need to make money. Even then, be cautious. Four out of five investors in options lose money.

Become your own options analyst

Overview

The methods of fundamental and technical analysis that you have learnt from this book will be useful when you select options, as you should be assessing and valuing the underlying stock.

Also watch Put–Call ratios. When there are many buyers of Calls on equities – leading to a low Put–Call ratio, a reversal is likely soon.

Conversely, when many investors are buying Puts – leading to a high Put–Call ratio – a few buyers will probably emerge to send the market soaring again.

How an option is priced

It is buyers and sellers who ultimately set the price of an option. From a theoretical perspective, City traders use a computerized version of the Black-Scholes model to value options. The model is based on the work of two US academics, Fisher Black and Myron Scholes, and was first published in 1973.

The mathematical formula for the Black-Scholes model is complex. In basic terms, it takes into account the intrinsic value of the option, its time value, and the fact that it does not pay dividends. The option's value is likely to rise with lower interest rates because investors need proportionately less incentive to use cash from deposit accounts to buy. The more volatile the underlying share price, the bigger are the chances of a big price swing in your favour, which increases the value of the option accordingly.

The weakness of the Black-Scholes model is that it assumes that the stock price moves randomly. It is based on the efficient market hypothesis that assumes stock prices reflect the full knowledge and expectations of investors. In practice, this is sometimes wrong.

The controversial Long Term Capital Management (LTCM), an investment fund founded by legendary ex-Salomon Brothers trader John Meriwether, relied partly on the Black-Scholes model to manage its assets using aggressive derivatives strategies, and Myron Scholes was one of its principal shareholders. When Meriwether was asked if he believed in efficient markets, he replied: 'I *make* them efficient'.

LTCM worked well in its early stages, offering shareholders a 42.8 per cent return in 1995, 40.8 per cent in 1996 and 17.1 per cent in 1997. In 1998, the fund memorably failed and was bailed out by the US Federal Reserve.

In less than extreme market conditions, Black-Scholes still tends to work better than alternative formulas, and so continues in use. But it is never perfect. If as an investor you can spot anomalies in value among options that have been priced according to the formula, you can make money.

Brokers and price data

You can trade options via the Internet through firms that specialize in options, but these sometimes place restrictions on you. Some brokers such as Sucden (www.sucden.co.uk) want minimum deposits. Others will take trades only by telephone.

Options Direct (www.mybroker.co.uk) suffers from neither of these limitations and is a popular choice. For other suitable brokers, visit the Web site of LIFFE (www.liffe.co.uk).

You will need price data. Sometimes your broker will provide this online. LIFFE (www.liffe.co.uk) offers you 15-minute-delayed prices.

Online learning and research

In this section, we have looked briefly at how options work. If you decide to explore this area of investment further, the Internet is your friend. But surf selectively, as many sites on options are designed to sell you expensive software or courses.

First, check out The Chicago Board Options Exchange (www.cboe.com). This site gives you a superbly readable, if uncontroversial, course on options. Despite the US slant, it is a good place to start learning.

In the UK, LIFFE offers a comprehensive online course covering options at www.liffe.co.uk. In addition, Berkeley Futures (www.bfl.co.uk) has a useful starter guide: *Everything you need to know about futures and options, but were afraid to ask*. Also helpful is the Siroc site (www.siroc.co.uk).

Make sure you visit the site of Shaeffersresearch.com (www.shaeffersresearch.com). This gives you an outstanding and fascinating overview on options, including how they work, how they are priced, and similar.

For ongoing coverage of options and other derivatives, use Marketeye (www.marketeye.com – accessed through www.thomsonfn.com). Also, subscribe to the weekly Options Review (£125 for 48 issues) published for private investors by stockbroker Charles Schwab (www.schwab-worldwide.com).

Warrants

Warrants are designed almost entirely for the private investor, which means that if you invest in this area, you are not competing with high-powered institutional investors. There are plenty of bargains to be snapped up.

Despite this, warrants, of which there are more than 160 traded on the London Stock Exchange, are more complicated than equities. They are risky investments, and should only form a small part of your portfolio.

If in doubt, stay out of warrants, at least until you have mastered some of the simpler areas of share dealing. If you are not put off, this is how they work.

Warrants entitle the holder to buy a specified number of shares in an underlying company at a specified exercise price at a particular time (or during a period) in the future. They do not form part of a company's share capital and so carry no voting rights. Warrants are sometimes compared with traded options, but differ in that they give the right to buy a *new* share from the company, while the option gives the right to buy an *existing* share from its owner.

If your shares do well or badly, it is likely that your warrants will follow suit. In percentage terms, warrants, as highly geared instruments, will rise and fall in value in line with the underlying shares, sometimes exaggerating the movements slightly. In absolute terms, the warrants make much bigger moves because they are much lower priced.

In currency terms, when you buy warrants, they will usually be in euros. However, the price of the underlying shares may be in an overseas currency and so affected by fluctuations in the foreign exchange rate. For capital gains tax purposes, warrants are aggregated with the shares subscribed.

Dealing in warrants

You can deal in warrants through your broker, but find one that understands them. You will be required to sign a risk warning, and your broker may have minimum dealing levels.

Before you commit yourself, check the basics. Find out for how many shares each warrant allows you to subscribe, the conversion date (typically several years ahead) and the conversion price. Some warrants have different conversion dates and prices, while others are less flexible.

Note the warrant's intrinsic value, which is how far the underlying company's share price is above the warrant's exercise price. Also note the premium, which is how much more you must initially pay for your warrant than it is worth on conversion.

The premium includes time value. The longer the time until expiry of the warrant, the more chance you have of converting the warrant at a profit. Time value declines sharply as the expiry date approaches, after which the warrant is worthless.

Most private investors prefer not to exercise warrants, but simply to trade them, which they must do before the expiry date. Usually, the warrants will expire worthless. But sometimes, on expiry, the company appoints a trustee to exercise the outstanding warrants and to sell the shares so gained, distributing their cash value to the original warrant holders.

Take advice from an expert

If you are interested in warrants, subscribe to the newsletter *Warrants Alert*, which has offered advice on UK equity warrants since 1989. It is written in a punchy but serious style, with an ear-to-the-ground editorial emphasis. It provides market comment and statistics, and assesses which warrants are technically over- or under-valued.

You can gain access to details of this newsletter, and some related advice on warrants, from the Web site www.tipsheets.co.uk. For general advice, also visit the warrants Web pages of Commerzbank (www.warrants.commerzbank.com).

Dynamic rules of the Online Share Buyer's FlexiSystem

- Options are highly geared financial instruments. In absolute terms, you will commit less money to options than you would by investing in the underlying securities. However, in percentage terms, you will see greater percentage gains and losses.
- You can trade options as a speculative investment, or use them to hedge your position.

- To check how cheaply options are priced, apply conventional valuation techniques to the underlying shares, and watch Put–Call ratios.
- You can exploit value anomalies in options that were priced on the Black-Scholes formula.
- Use the Internet for further research into options. Start by visiting the Web site of The Chicago Board Options Exchange (www.cboe.com).
- Warrants are a market for amateurs, which means that there are bargains available.
- Warrants are risky, and should form only a small part of your portfolio. If in doubt, stay out.
- You can deal in warrants through your stockbroker, but find one that understands them.
- Buy warrants at the lowest possible premium. Note the intrinsic value, which is how far the underlying share price is above the warrant's exercise price.
- You will usually trade rather than exercise warrants.
- The best source of information on warrants is the newsletter *Warrants Alert*. You can find out more from the Web site www.tipsheets.co.uk.

Day 10

The daredevil trader: financial futures, spread betting, CFDs and forex

Overview

In this module we will first look at financial futures. We will focus on spread betting, which is a popular way to trade futures. We shall then look at contracts for difference, and Universal Futures Contracts. Finally, we will survey forex trading opportunities online. For all these high risk/high reward areas, I will recommend appropriate dealers and online resources.

Financial futures

The futures market deals in contracts, which are agreements between two parties to buy and sell the underlying instrument in a specific quantity at a pre-arranged date at an agreed price. The contracts can be for commodities such as corn, steel, beef or cocoa. In all cases, this is a paper investment, and you will never have to take delivery of the underlying product. Contracts can also be for financial instruments, which is what we will be focusing on in this module. Contracts in, for example, interest rates or stock market indices are available on the London International Financial Futures & Options Exchange (www.liffe.co.uk). Trades are passed to the London Clearing House that arranges fulfilment of the contract.

If you trade in financial futures, you will be speculating on the price of your chosen instrument rising or falling in the future. Alternatively you will be hedging, by which you will aim to compensate for potential losses elsewhere with profits on your futures. The markets are highly liquid and commission charges are small in relation to the deal size.

As a trader, you need put up only a proportion of the value of the contract as initial margin. In this way, futures are highly geared, so you can make or lose much more than you have put up. This concept will be familiar to you from traded options (see Day 9), which, incidentally, are available on many futures contracts.

As with options, if the futures contract moves against you, you will need to pay variation margin (extra money up front) to hold your position open. Many successful traders never pay this but simply close out their position and take losses. Also, most traders use stop loss orders (see Day 4) to lock in their profits or minimize losses.

One popular way to invest in futures is through financial spread betting, a fast-growing industry which we will look at in the next few paragraphs.

Spread betting

How spread betting works

In financial spread betting, you can place a bet with a bookmaker based on your belief that a share price, an index, interest rates or similar will move in a certain direction. Most financial spread bets are on futures or options which, by *anticipating* movements, are likely to move faster than the underlying financial instrument.

The dealer will quote you a two-way price, not knowing whether you are buying or selling. You may then place your bet, nominating a unit stake which is typically £2–£5 on small transactions, per single point.

You will pay up-front only 10–15 per cent of the sum you are betting, which is useful if you are short of liquid funds. This is another example of investing on margin, where you stand to gain or lose much more than you put up. Once you hold a credit account with a bookmaker, you may be able to avoid making any up-front payment.

The spread on any transaction – the difference between the buying and selling prices – must be covered before you are in a position to make a profit. You can limit your losses by a stop loss, which you can apply personally or, more reliably, have built into your bet.

When you close out your position, you will receive your winnings or pay your losses. The difference between the price at which you placed your bet and that at which you close it out will be your profit or loss.

How much does spread betting cost you?

You will pay neither commissions nor fees to the financial bookmaker. The firm makes its money entirely from the spread, which includes betting tax, expenses, and the firm's profit margin. The more liquid the market in the financial instrument on which you are betting, the narrower is the spread.

In financial spread betting, you will not pay the stamp duty on purchases that is required on conventional share purchases.

Your profits are free of capital gains tax, and you need not declare them to the Inland Revenue. The flip side is that you cannot offset your losses against capital gains elsewhere.

Any time, any place

You can bet on a wide range of instruments, including options and interest rates, as well as individual shares in the UK, continental Europe and the United States. You can also punt on a variety of indices, most commonly the FTSE-100 or the Dow Jones but also the TechMARK 100 or a sectoral index. You can also play the foreign exchange (forex) market, which we will look at separately later in this module.

In addition, you can take out a grey market bet on the price at which companies that are going to float will start trading in the secondary market. You can bet on company results, and on key City votes such as, at the time of writing, the demutualization of Standard Life.

You can place your bet over the Internet, or by e-mail, as well as by phone. You can often do so out of market hours. If so, this will typically be more expensive. As in any business activity, you must try to keep your costs down, and this means controlling your risk.

Control your risk

If you plan to speculate in spread betting, set aside some capital for the purpose that you can afford to lose. Start by making some small bets as you get used to the market. Bet on large popular financial instruments such as the FTSE 100 index where the spreads tend to be narrower.

Never feel that you have to bet if conditions do not seem right. Stockbroker and spread betting expert Charles Vintcent told investors at a recent London conference: 'The usual mistake people make in spread betting is that they bet too often. Watch the market and bet small amounts regularly. You'll never make a living out of it, but you'll pay for your holidays and have fun.'

Stop losses and limit orders

For your peace of mind when you place a bet, it makes sense to use a stop loss, as this sets a limit on your losses. Be warned that a financial instrument can fall too fast for you to apply the stop at the set percentage level.

The reliable alternative is to use a *guaranteed* stop (unavailable on traded options), which the spread betting firm undertakes will apply when losses reach a set percentage level. If you have this facility on your bet, expect the spread to be wider.

Consider also using a limit order, which enables you to close a bet at a predetermined profit level. Some traders take out a stop loss and limit order at the same time, so defining the perimeters within which they will make a profit and loss.

A market mostly for speculators

As we have seen, spread betting is versatile. The cautious investor can hedge his position by betting that the share price or index in which they are conventionally invested will go the opposite way. If this should happen, the gain on the bet would at least partly compensate for the downside on the investment.

In practice, it is mostly speculators who are attracted to spread betting. About a third of clients of spread betting firms work in the City of London. These people have more understanding of financial markets than most, and some have money to burn. They are tempted to take risks for short-term gain.

More often than not the spread betting firm wins out. I have seen punters lose tens of thousands of pounds very quickly in this game, sometimes on one deal. Less often, I have seen them gain as much. One of the riskiest and least understood areas of spread betting is selling short, which is popular in falling markets.

Selling short

To sell short is to sell an investment that you do not own that you will buy back later, at a profit, you hope, to meet with the requirement to deliver the shares. This bearish investment technique is no longer realistic in conventional share trading except over an extremely short period, due to short settlement periods. It can be, and is, still done through spread betting.

A safer bet, if you have the technology and the time, and can move quickly, is arbitrage.

Arbitrage

Arbitrage is when you make a profit based on the difference in the spread on the same bet offered by two respective bookmakers.

I know of one individual who made £160,000 from such arbitraging over an eight-month period, using three screens and two telephones, with a mobile phone as back-up. He would capitalize on small two or three point differentials in spreads, buying through one bookmaker and selling immediately through another.

If you become known as an arbitrageur, financial bookmakers are likely to limit their dealings with you. Otherwise, they want your business, even if it is small.

Select the right financial bookmaker

Some spread betting firms try to entice you into opening an account with them, even if you are a complete novice. Some firms will invite you into their offices for coffee evenings, and individuals will speak at privately organized seminars where spread betting novices learn their trade.

The temptation is strong, but do not be persuaded to start spread betting until you feel comfortable with the risk and the pace. Also, be selective over your choice of financial bookmaker. Most firms offering bets in the UK are authorized by the Securities and Futures Association (SFA), which offers you some comeback if anything goes wrong, but firms do not all offer the same bets and, when they do, their spreads may vary slightly.

First, decide what you want to bet on, and then find a suitable financial bookmaker, comparing spreads on offer for the same deal (you will find a list in the Appendix). If you want a punt on the FTSE-100 index, you will have a good choice of firms. If you want to place a more unusual bet, you might do best to go to IG Index, which is the longest established firm and offers a wider range of bets than the rest. If you want to place a low size bet, Financial Spreads is a good firm to use.

Web resources

There is a wealth of information about spread betting on the Internet, but tread carefully. I know of a financial fraudster who served a sentence in a young offenders' institution, and who came out and set up various financial rackets. His most recent venture is into the world of spread betting consultancy, and he is involved in a Web site that focuses on this area.

In selling his services, he produces paperwork that provides apparent evidence of his huge wins on spread betting based on his understanding of financial markets. In reality, this is a scam.

He obtains this evidence by placing enormous bets through two spread betting firms at once, each on opposite ways. If the market shifts significantly, one bet will gain heavily, and the other lose by as much. At this point, he will sell out of both bets, breaking even except for the costs incurred from the spreads.

He will photocopy only the paperwork representing the *winning* bet and mail this to his potential clients as apparent cast-iron evidence of his successful recent track record in financial spread betting. He repeats the trick regularly, representing himself as a guru with the Midas touch.

I am telling you this true story to warn you about the risks of paying for tipping services. Web sites are increasingly offering this, and my advice is to steer clear. Unscrupulous operators make a more reliable profit from giving advice on spread betting than from practising it. The advice may be good but, if it is not, you will lose not just your subscription fees but also from the bets that you place.

But use the Internet to learn about spread betting. Go first to Onewaybet.com (www.onewaybet.com), which is the independent Web site run by Angus McCrone, an economist and spread betting journalist who writes regularly for the London *Evening Standard*. This site has tables comparing spreads and sizes of bets from financial bookmakers. It also has quality educational material, and is updated regularly. In my view, it is the best of its kind.

You can also learn about spread betting from the Web site of The Internet Sporting Club (www.internetsportingclub.co.uk), an online tipsheet. You will find the broad concept well explained at spreadbetting explained (www.spreadbettingexplained.com), and at spreadbets.net (www.spreadbets.net).

Financial bookmakers as well as futures brokers are likely to deal also in contracts for difference (CFDs), another market that speculators love.

Contracts for difference

A CFD is an agreement between two parties to exchange the difference between the opening and closing price of a contract, multiplied by the specified number of shares, as calculated at the contract's close.

CFDs are available on the top 350 stocks in the UK, as well as on selected stocks in continental Europe and the United States. By investing in a CFD, you are not the registered owner of the underlying share, so you will not have shareholders' voting rights or access to product discounts. However, you are entitled to dividend payments.

You can trade CFDs on the Internet or by telephone, and will need an initial deposit of at least £10,000. CFDs are suitable for experienced investors. UK-based brokers will accept your business only on the basis that you understand the significant risks.

Like spread bets, CFDs are highly geared. You will buy on margin, putting up 10–25 per cent of your total investment, and effectively borrowing the rest from your broker. You will need to meet margin calls (marking to market), initially from cash deposited in advance.

The broker will charge commission on CFD deals, or will take its cut from the spread. The firm will also charge interest on the amount that you borrow in striking a purchase (taking a long position). The flip side is that it will pay interest once you have gone short on a position (for which CFDs, like spread bets, are ideal).

In either case, interest is usually slightly above base rate, and is recalculated daily. You will not pay stamp duty on your CFD purchase, but will be liable for capital gains tax on your profits. You can hold your position open in CFDs indefinitely, subject to paying margin calls and interest on loans. But more typically, they are a short-term trading proposition.

Common trading strategies

You can use CFDs to your advantage where a fast gain may be possible, and for hedging purposes. Let me explain two such trading situations.

The first is to buy CFDs in stocks that are expected to enter the FTSE-100 index when its constituents are reviewed every quarter. At this point, companies with a market capitalization below the 110th place are relegated from the index, and others join it.

If you are to follow this strategy, you should buy a relevant CFD a few days before the index entrants are formally announced. You should sell the CFD the night before the stock enters the FTSE as, at this point, the share price often drops. In parallel, you could short stocks likely to be relegated from the FTSE-100 and then reverse your position. To keep abreast of changes in the FTSE-100 index, visit the FTSE International Web site (www.ftse.com).

The second strategy is dual trading, also known as spread trading. This is when you invest in the performance of one stock against another. You may buy a CFD in a stock that seems a likely out-performer, and simultaneously go short on a stock that you think is overvalued. Traders often choose two stocks from the same sector that have historically reacted to the same industry issues and news. Using this strategy, you will broadly maintain a market neutral position. You will benefit from any share price rise in the stock you have backed for out-performance, while reducing the downside risk.

Choose the right broker

When choosing your broker or bookmaker from the many available, look for fast execution of deals, competitive costs and access to high quality research. For a list of some dealers in CFDs, see the Appendix. Let us here compare a few examples.

CMC Group (www.deal4free.com) is one of the originators of commission-free CFD dealing, with all charges built into the spread. This is a user-friendly dealing service. Visit the company's Web site and you will find such facilities as a calculator to compare CFDs with ordinary shares in terms of trading costs, and a regular commentary from a technical analysis perspective.

Another established player is Berkeley Futures (www.bfl.co.uk), which offers its clients advice on trading strategies in CFDs, and access to a real trading room. GNI (www.gni.co.uk), another leading player, is known for its excellent research facilities. It offers daily market comment and a technical analyst's perspective, as well as a Sunday newspaper round-up. It has a table of the top 150 UK companies by market capitalization, which you can use for forecasting candidates for leaving and joining the FTSE 100 in the quarterly review (see Common trading strategies above).

Further information

You will find a very good explanation of how CFDs work at Sucden UK (www.equitycfd.co.uk) and at IGIndex Direct (www.igshares.com). Also check out Copperchip (www.copperchip.co.uk).

Universal futures contracts (UFCs)

Competition for CFDs

The London International Financial Futures Exchange (LIFFE) launched its Universal Futures Contracts (UFCs) in early 2001. It kicked off with 25 European and US blue chips, including France Telecom, Deutsche Bank and Microsoft.

UFCs are comparable to CFDs, although less flexible, and dealing may turn out to be cheaper. They have regulated clearing, through LIFFE, and offer a simple, low-cost way to gain exposure to international stocks.

Despite this, UFCs are currently of greater interest to institutional than private investors, although this balance is likely to change. For more information, visit the LIFFE Web site (www.liffe.com).

Firms that will trade UFCs online include Easy2Trade (www.easy2trade.com), ManDirect (www.mandirect.co.uk) and Options Direct (www.mybroker.co.uk).

Foreign exchange (forex)

An accessible market

The Internet has made the forex market accessible to many private investors (see also under spread betting earlier in this module). Although it is not strictly investing, forex trading has particular appeal for those who trade derivatives as it offers similar high gearing, and some volatility.

The forex market has other advantages. It has no shortage of buyers and sellers, and its participants can operate over the telephone worldwide. This market is too large for traders to manipulate it easily. It is open 24 hours per day, with two-day settlement on trades.

As a trader in this high-risk market, you will buy one currency and sell another, hoping to profit on the turn. In every deal there is a base currency and an exchange currency. The most popular trades include those between the US dollar and either sterling or the euro.

Spot and forward rates

The spot rate (cash price) is the current exchange rate at which you can trade one currency for another. There is also a forward rate, which applies when you enter a forward contract to buy a currency at a prearranged price on a given future date.

What moves the forex market

Macroeconomic factors have a major influence on the forex market. If, for example, the UK raises its interest rates, this attracts investors to the country, and sterling accordingly rises in value. Macro-economic changes can be slow, and forex market trends are more stable than on some financial markets.

Many forex traders use technical analysis to aid trading decisions. For this reason, it is worth getting to grips with the basics covered on Day 5, although you will have to adapt your skills to the forex context.

Find the right firm for your forex trading

To find a forex trader on the Internet, visit the comprehensive directory at www.digitallook.com. Included here are some firms that deal on the Internet and by telephone. In the UK, some of the big names are ED&F Man (www.edfman.com), Sucden (www.sucden.co.uk), GNI (www.gni.co.uk) and Cantor Fitzgerald International (www.cantor.com). In the United States, check out Lind-Waldock (www.lind-waldock.com).

News and research

There is a surfeit of forex news and research on the Internet. Some is available free, but much only on subscription. Check out Trend Analysis (www.trend-analysis.com), which is an independent service offering reports on currency movements. Forexia (www.gen-fx.com/forexia.htm), the independent research house, produces a good newsletter.

The way forward

The financial instruments covered in this module are mainly of interest to speculators and hedgers. Before you get involved, make sure that you have experience of trading and investment, and understand the risks.

Dynamic rules of the Online Share Buyer's FlexiSystem

- Financial spread betting is a highly geared form of speculation on the future performance of a wide range of financial instruments. You can also place bets for hedging purposes. Use only

capital you can afford to lose and apply a stop loss. Any profits are free of capital gains tax.
- CFDs are similarly highly geared. They charge interest on your position, and any profits are subject to capital gains tax.
- UFCs are a less flexible but low cost alternative to CFDs. They are backed by LIFFE.
- The forex market has high gearing and some volatility, and is highly liquid. Macro-economic factors are a major driving force.

Day 11
Alternatives to online dealing

Overview

Most online brokers are execution-only, which means that they do not give you specific investment advice. The main alternative is the traditional advisory broker. In this module, I will advise on how to select an advisory broker, and how these firms may operate compared with their online counterparts.

I have seen investors lose money to advisory brokers so often that I have decided to use this module to give you a no-holds-barred insight into how the shadier firms operate. I will explain their dubious sales techniques, and the notorious pump-and-dump routine.

As a starting investor, you are all too likely to come across the sharks. There are also plenty of respectable advisory brokers, but they are not always so interested in small clients.

Alternatives to an online broker

If, after reading this book, you do not feel quite ready to use an online broker, consider one of the following two alternatives.

The discretionary account route

Should you have a sizeable sum to invest, you can open a discretionary account where the broker will make all the buying and selling decisions for you. If you do, keep an eye on what your broker is doing with your money.

The advisory broker route

If you want advice on your investment decisions, which most online brokers do not provide, consider opening an account with an advisory broker. The charges will be higher than an online dealer's. However, a good broker will steer you from the poor buying and selling decisions that you may otherwise make from inexperience. In this module, we will be looking mainly at advisory brokers.

How to select an advisory broker

In general, you need an experienced individual within the firm who will take time and trouble with you. If your account is small, such a service will be easier to find in the provinces than in or around London. Provincial broking firms are also more likely to take on new clients.

A firm that suits one person may not suit another. Before you start dealing with a broker, investigate the background and track record of both the firm and the individual with whom you will be dealing. Find out his or her favoured investment strategy and make sure that it fits with your own. If, for instance, you like to buy and hold blue chips, you have no use for a broker who prefers to trade small, speculative stocks.

Unfortunately, many advisory brokers try to trade client accounts as much as possible to generate commission. These pirates have no regard for your investment needs, although they will pretend otherwise. If your broker keeps losing you money on stocks, find a new firm.

Even if you trust your broker, never rely on his or her tips entirely. Ask searching questions, conduct your own research, and do not buy until you are satisfied that you are making the right investment. At the very least, read about individual stocks on the message boards of the Motley Fool UK Web site (www.fool.co.uk) under the A–Z index for stocks. This will tell you how the stock has done recently, and what current shareholders feel about it.

In the next few pages, I will provide what you will get from nobody else, an insider's guide to games that some of the less scrupulous advisory brokers play. *Not all brokers operate in these ways.* Even if he or she is working for a poorly resourced firm, an advisory broker could be doing well for you if he or she has a good instinct for the market, and is attempting to act in your interest.

Of the dubious brokers, please note that many are not as bad as in the examples I am about to show you, although some are worse. As I will make clear, if you use an online broker, you can avoid the more damaging chicanery.

Dubious advisory brokers' tricks

The cunningly qualified recommendation

Dubious advisory brokers are ever the optimists. They represent the stock they are pushing as special, and the market as always going up. At the same time, they cover their position so that, if the share price subsequently collapses, buyers cannot claim that they have been misled.

These brokers will have been taught in their trainee days never to say that a stock *will*, or is *certain to*, rise in value. Instead, they must qualify their statement and say that the stock *should*, or *is likely to*, rise in value. This way, victims of their sales pitch will later find it much harder to accuse them of giving misleading information.

Once the client has decided to buy a large number of shares on the strength of such a sales pitch, the broker may cover him- or herself further by saying something like: 'Of course, I can't make any guarantees about any stock – you understand that?' and pause for the client's consent, before continuing with: 'With that proviso, I have great hopes for this one...'

The client is unlikely to backtrack on his or her buying decision. Generally, he or she decides whether, and how much, to invest more on the broker's telephone manner and tone of voice than on the literal meaning of his or her words.

Online brokers compared

When you buy and sell shares online, you are not exposed to a telephone presence and pushed into buying shares on the spot. Online, stocks are hyped only in print, which leaves you in control.

Tricks to keep your capital invested

As a medium- to long-term investor, you should adopt a buy-and-hold strategy on shares. At the same time, apply common sense. When the stock market sets into temporary decline, you may do best to sell your shares, and buy back later at a lower price. If you have bought new issues, you will often do best to sell immediately after flotation (see Day 7).

In all such cases, the dubious advisory broker prefers you not to sell, unless you buy other shares from him or her at the same time. The broker wants control over your money. If you were to sell shares for cash, you might eventually reinvest somewhere, and the broker fears that this could be away from him or her.

For this reason, your advisory broker may use various tricks to keep you from selling a stock. I know of one broker who responds to client sell requests with: 'You must be out of your mind. You should be buying more'. Often then, the clients will double up their holdings. The brokers know that the need to sell stock is often less than clients claim.

Alternatively, brokers may say: 'Don't sell *that* one', implying that they know of major developments within the company, but cannot reveal them. 'If you sell, you will lose out on a big share price rise', the broker suggests. This will all be kept vague, so that there can be no accusation later that the broker has made misleading statements.

If you prove insistent on selling, the broker may ask you to wait for just another couple of weeks – during which, he or she implies, the company's fortunes may take a turn for the better. 'If you then still wish to sell, go ahead,' you will be told. If you agree to this, the broker knows that there is a good chance that after a few days you will have dismissed the whole matter from your mind. As an added disincentive, the broker may put the onus on *you* to ring up about selling the stock. If you call, the broker may be unavailable.

Online brokers compared

Online, you will find it as easy to sell stock as to buy it. There is no pressure on you to reinvest the capital.

The one-sided case

The dubious broker presents news and research selectively to back his or her sales case. He or she cites only positive stock valuations regardless of the overall picture.

If a stock has performed poorly, the broker will say that it is undervalued, and stress the low PE ratio (see Day 3). In this case, the broker will cite studies showing that companies with low PE ratios have historically outperformed the market, but will not point out that they cover a long period that includes some individual years of under-performance. The broker will not let it slip that a low PE ratio often reflects poor prospects.

Conversely, if the broker is selling a growth stock with a high PE ratio, he or she will stress the benefits of relative strength and cite studies showing that stocks that outperformed in the past have more often than not continued to do so.

Brokers in some of the more dubious firms have access to little or no in-house research. The least well-informed are the half-commission brokers, so-called because they split commissions earned on their own stock deals with their firm. Some of these brokers obtain their share recommendations second-hand, from either the out-of-date research reports of other firms or, worse still, press tips.

Online brokers compared

The well-known online brokers never push dubious stocks, although some are involved in high-risk share offerings.

Some Internet promoters push dubious stocks, but without putting immediate pressure on you to buy on the telephone. You can make your decision in a more relaxed way, after conducting your own research on the Web.

The concealed churn

Dubious brokers will *churn* your portfolio. This means that they will buy and sell shares for you with the sole aim of generating commission for themselves. Churning is in breach of the Financial Services Act, and the broker who is caught is likely to attract the attention of the City regulators.

The so-called *concealed* or *disguised* churn gives the unscrupulous broker a loophole. Using this technique, the broker manipulates the private investor into making what he or she thinks is his or her *own* decision to sell part of the portfolio and use the proceeds to buy new shares.

The broker will deliver a sales pitch that is something like this: 'This small high-tech stock has never been at such a low price. That's why a lot of City professionals are quietly buying it up. Of course I couldn't *recommend* that you sell your blue-chip shares to get involved. This is technically a speculative investment. While I know what I would do in your shoes, you must make your own decision.'

On such prompting from an experienced rogue broker, experience shows that eight clients out of ten will sell good stocks to reinvest in speculative rubbish. Just before executing the trade, the broker will reiterate that the decision is the client's and that there is a risk involved. In his or her own interest, the broker is likely to be taping all calls.

In this style, I know of one broker who dealt with a client – a school caretaker who had inherited some money for investing – up to six times a day for some months. The caretaker came in and out of supposed hot high-tech stocks, gradually losing more and more money. The City considered that the individual broker was behaving acceptably as, technically, he had explained the risks and was acting on the client's instructions.

The better technology spiral

The more speculative a stock, the more likely it is to be dubiously sold. In particular watch out for the *better technology* vicious circle into which unscrupulous brokers tap during a bull market.

The broker will start the ball rolling almost imperceptibly. Soon after you have bought into one high-tech stock, the broker will suggest, sometimes indirectly, that its technology has become outdated, then try to prompt you into selling the stock, reinvesting the proceeds in a company that he or she represents as more technologically advanced.

Investors moved by such exhortations may sell shares in wire line telephone companies and reinvest the proceeds in cable technology. They will then jump ship for fibre optics. Whatever technologies are available now, there is always a newer version that has not yet been released. Unfortunately, not all new technologies are better than the old, and the companies that use them are not all equal. If you know little about the technology market, your broker may try to exploit your ignorance.

Online brokers compared

The online broker cannot churn your account in this way. At worst, online dealing is so easy that you are tempted to churn your *own* portfolio. Again, however, you will be in control.

Covering up ignorance

Advisory brokers often know nothing. Most will have passed the Registered Persons exam that is compulsory for stockbrokers who make share recommendations to the public. But this is a very simple multiple choice paper – prepared for in a few weeks and instantly forgettable. Some brokers hold the Securities Institute Diploma, which is considerably more advanced than the Registered Persons exam, but is undemanding compared with professional exams of doctors, solicitors and similar.

Many come from backgrounds unrelated to financial services. I personally know brokers who had until recently been bar staff, taxi drivers, double glazing salespeople, burger bar assistants, and so on.

When dubious brokers do not know the answer to questions, they may cover up. They will never admit their ignorance. Instead they will say something like: 'Hang on please, I've just got a call coming in from the States'. The client will be put on hold while the broker checks the query with somebody more knowledgeable. Then the broker will say: 'Sorry about that. What was your question?' The client will repeat it, and the broker will provide the right answer as if spontaneously.

Alternatively, the brokers may evade the question altogether. If, for example, a client asks why a company's earnings fell, the broker might parry with: 'That's unimportant for the company at this stage. What counts is revenue'.

The bottom line is that brokers are successful in their new profession if they trade plenty of stock, regardless of whether you make money. If you do not, they will blame market conditions, or other unforeseen events.

Online brokers compared

The online broker will typically provide an e-mail and perhaps a telephone facility to handle your queries. But these facilities are often inadequate, and the firm may be understaffed.

Targeted dubious stock promotions

Targeted dubious stock promotions used to be the speciality of licensed dealers in securities. These firms were a downmarket alternative to stockbrokers. Many closed down shortly after the Financial Services Act was implemented in early 1988. Some survived into the 1990s. A few, in a revamped form, are around today.

These bucket shops have a reputation for hard-selling stocks. They have in particular cornered the market for penny shares, which have an irresistible appeal for private investors. For more about this specialist market, see Day 6.

The most notorious of these firms have always operated abroad where they can usually escape retributive action from UK victims of their scams. Some still work in hide-outs in one country, but receive calls via a switching office in another. This way, they keep their whereabouts secret. As they are also operating under false names, they will never be easily traced.

The bucket shop will typically offer speculative shares to its private clients at a normal price. If the underlying company is quoted on a recognized exchange, its shares may retail at slightly below the market price, which makes them seem a bargain to unsophisticated investors.

In reality, the firm recommends the shares not because they are a good deal, as it claims, but because it wants to get rid of them at a higher price than it bought them, as quickly as possible. In this initiative, the firm considers only its own interests. Any of its clients who buy the stock may find not only that it is a poor performer, but also that they become victims of the infamous pump-and-dump routine.

The pump-and-dump manoeuvre

The pump-and-dump is a calculated manoeuvre in which planning starts early. The share dealing firm may retain a significant chunk of shares on its books of a stock that it is pushing. In addition, associates of the firm may buy shares through nominee accounts.

Next, the firm's salespeople will push the stock onto private clients. It is likely to be small, with a thin market for its shares, in which case the concentrated sales campaign should send the share price soaring.

The spread – the difference between the buying and selling price – may be as high as 25 per cent. Buyers would need to see the stock rise by more than this if they are to sell out at a profit. However, once the share price exceeds the spread, the salespeople will advise existing shareholders to buy more.

As the surge of buying reaches a frenzy, the share pushers may dump their own holdings at a vast profit, causing a sudden plunge in the share price as a result of the excess stock that will have hit the market. The investors who recently bought will rush to sell.

They will find that it is not so easy. The bid price that they are quoted will be for only a very small number of shares, and will fall dramatically if they try to sell more. Many will make the most common mistake of all. Encouraged by their broker, they will hold rather than sell, watching in dismay from the sidelines as their shares continue to plummet in value.

The one-off sting

The one-off stock scam is a particularly insidious version of the pump and dump. Rogue dealers will ring clients with whom the firm has dealt fairly over a period and so built up trust. They will offer these clients a quick in-and-out on a private placing of a speculative stock, very likely an unknown high-tech or oil and gas company. The company will typically be based abroad.

The dealer may send out a prospectus. This will have some unrealistic profits and cash-flow projections, and will be full of warnings. The company may have no revenues, let alone profits. But many clients will not be warned off.

'You will be in and out within a month', the broker may say, and will promise clients a small profit on the short term transaction – big enough to entice them, but not enough to make them suspicious. To release capital for investing in the stock, clients will empty their building societies, and cash in unit trusts and blue-chip stocks.

After buying the new stock, they may never be able to sell out, but this will not be immediately apparent. The broker will cite market conditions, or, if the stock originates from outside the UK, perhaps the exchange rate, as a reason for clients to hold the stock for longer than the month originally envisaged.

Typically, the only market maker for the stock will be the broker who sold it in the first place. If the firm refuses to buy back, the stock will be worthless. The firm may offer an alternative to holding the stock indefinitely. Clients may be allowed to sell out, only if they will immediately reinvest the proceeds (and more) into another equally dubious stock. This is a pointless exercise.

Eventually clients' faith will be shattered. Before this happens, the firm will push dubious stocks hard. It may launch so-called dog-and-pony clients' evenings in top London hotels, and invite dupes into luxury offices for a spectacular lunch over which the brokers make their sales pitch.

You may ask how such a situation could be allowed to arise in the first place. Typically, an unscrupulous firm takes over a struggling but basically honest company and uses its good name to push dubious stocks onto its long-established clients.

Before anybody realizes what has happened, it is too late. The new owner will fight regulators and clients in every way, buying time until the firm eventually ceases trading. By this stage, the principals will have skipped the country, if they had ever been in it, leaving their highly paid lackeys to carry the can.

Online brokers compared

The Internet is a hotbed of pump-and-dump stock promotions, including one-off hits. The Web is inadequately policed and, unless you have an experienced eye, it is not easy to spot the duds. Dubious Internet and other high-tech companies are young, loss-making, and have limited revenues, but so are their *bona fide* counterparts. A professional-looking Web site set up by crooks bamboozles a surprising number of investors.

Have nothing to do with unknown stock promoters that operate over the Internet. Do not even register with their Web sites. In addition, if a salesman from an unknown firm rings you cold and tries to sell you shares, slam down the telephone receiver.

Let me at this point alert you to Stock Detective, a US-based vigilante Web site that is now based at www.financialweb.com. It exposes and analyses stock promotion scams across the world but particularly in the United States and Canada. Visit the site also for background perspectives and insights.

If, despite the risks, you are *seriously* interested in a speculative stock pedalled by an unknown Internet promoter, first do your research. Check where the company is quoted – if anywhere –, as well as its history and financials. Find out the background of its principals.

Treat any cash flow and earnings protections, even if from a claimed independent source, with healthy scepticism. If in doubt, do not buy. If against my advice you buy on the basis of what you read on the Web, print out and file the relevant pages. They will be evidence if it turns out that you have been ripped off.

The way forward

Over the years, I have helped many UK investors who have suffered at the hands of share sharks. I am pleased to say that people are wising up. The proliferation of financial information, analysis and news flow on the Internet has undoubtedly helped the process.

By investing online, you will avoid the risk of having your savings milked by a less-than-scrupulous advisory broker. But you will still be faced with the problems of stock selection and deciding when to sell. Before you get involved on any scale, make sure that you have got to grips with this entire book.

Dynamic rules of the Online Share Buyer's FlexiSystem

- If you use a discretionary broker, watch how he invests your money.
- Select an advisory broker carefully. A firm with a good track record and a suitable investment strategy can help you. But there are some sharp operators.
- The dubious advisory broker trades your account excessively while making you think that you are making your own decisions.
- Avoid buying shares in small companies as a result of a concentrated sales campaign. You may become the victim of a pump-and-dump manoeuvre.
- Do not buy speculative shares from firms that you do not know or have not checked out.

Day 12

...s from reading

Geoff Muirhead CBE
Group Chief Executive
MAG

...elp to make you rich, provided that
y...   t their advice into practice, adapting
it to...   nd investment opportunities.

In this...   k first at the advantages of finding
out about, an...   ks online. I will introduce my two
favourite online...   Next, I will recommend some excellent
books that cover all t... r areas of online stock market investing.
I will include some fiction.

As I will explain, you can often read online reviews of a title that interests you before you commit your money. It is important that you spend time on books that are right for you. Your choice is a very personal thing, and will partly depend on how experienced an investor you are. Use these pages simply as a guideline.

The online advantage

Thanks to the Internet, finding out about and ordering books has never been easier. Online, you can look up individual titles, browse, read reviews and place orders for instant delivery at a discounted price. You may select from far more titles than are available in most bookshops.

Some online bookshops publish reviews on their Web site. This is useful, but the reviewers are sometimes friends of the author. Be sceptical. At the same time, if several readers have reviewed a book, you can usually gain an idea of what it is like from the composite picture – not least because some reviewers will react to earlier reviews.

On Amazon (www.amazon.co.uk), which is my favourite online bookshop, many books are reviewed. You can usually read a synopsis of the text and author's profile, as well as seeing a picture of the dust jacket, and details of the author's other books. The book will be given a sales ranking. You can find out what recent buyers of this title have also bought from Amazon, and look these up.

On the Web sites of Amazon, and Global Investor (www.globalinvestor.com), an excellent online financial bookshop, you can sometimes find an online interview with the author. On financial Web sites such as that of The Motley Fool, UK (www.fool.co.uk), you can browse through (and contribute to) discussion boards where readers discuss books.

You will find that the important business and investment books are mostly published by a small number of publishers, including, but not confined to, Kogan Page, John Wiley, FT Pearson, Orion and McGraw-Hill. Each of these publishers presents its books in a broadly uniform style.

Recommended books

Online investing

On online investing, there are surprisingly few good UK books for novices. Most of the books are from the United States, and place too much emphasis on technical analysis.

As a nuts-and-bolts introduction, there is not much to beat *Online Share Investing, a UK guide,* by Alistair Fitt, (Ftyourmoney.com, 2000). The author explains various approaches to investing, and the technicalities of dealing online. He favours value investing, and is cynical about technical analysis.

Another worthwhile beginners' book is *The Fool's Guide to Online Investing*, by Nigel Roberts with David Berger (Boxtree, 2000). This is written in the usual tongue-in-cheek style of the Motley Fool UK Web site. It will put off some readers, but will attract others.

Trading Online, by Alpesh Patel (Pearson Education, 2000), is written by a successful trader, which is an advantage in itself. The text is broken up into bite-size chunks, which makes for digestible, if sometimes superficial, reading. The book covers technical analysis comprehensively. An alternative primer presented in a more traditional way is *The New Online Investor* by Peter Temple (John Wiley, 2000). The book contains a wealth of detail about relevant Web sites.

Broader investing perspectives

For a broad overview of today's stock markets, read *Streetwise: Guide to Beating the Market and Investing with Confidence,* edited by Nils Pratley and Lorna Bourke (Hodder & Stoughton, 2000). The book was compiled by a number of journalists who worked for the now defunct financial Web site TheStreet.co.uk (see Day 1). The text contains perspectives on every aspect of investing, including the new economy.

For details on such mechanics of share ownership as annual general meetings, shareholders' circulars, and getting value from your broker, I recommend *The Shareholder* by Simon Rose (Mercury Business Books, 1991). This is written in the same irreverent style as the author's excellent stock market primer *Fair Shares* (Management Books, 2000).

Books that list Web sites

Books that list Web sites date, but can be a useful reference source. My favourite is *The UK Guide to Online Investing*, by Michael Scott (McGraw-Hill, 2000). Using large colour photographs, it guides you through some key financial Web sites. Other helpful handbooks include *The Sunday Times Guide to Money Online* by Matthew Wall (HarperCollins, 2000) and *The Top 200 Web Sites for Personal Finance* by Christina Daniels (Kogan Page, 2000).

For further guidance on choosing an online broker, go for *The UK Guide to Online Brokers* by Michael Scott (Investment Gateway, 2000). If you plan on investing outside the UK, I recommend *Investing Online*, by Stephen Eckett (FT Pitman Publishing, 1997). The book lists financial Web sites from countries around the world.

Share trading

On short-term share trading, a wonderful read is *Make a Million in Twelve Months* by James Hipwell and Anil Bhoyrul (John Blake, 2000). This is a lightweight book by two former *Daily Mirror* journalists. It shows you how to buy when the share price has fallen, and to sell when it has risen.

If day trading is your niche, read *Understand Day Trading in a Day*, by Ian Bruce (Take That, 2000). It explains the basics of setting up as a day trader and how markets work. It also provides an overview of technical analysis.

An entertaining account of online share buying is *How to Make Your Million from the Internet*, by Jonathan Maitland (Hodder & Stoughton, 2001). The author is a TV broadcaster who mortgaged his house for £50,000. He tried to turn this sum into £1 million over 12 months through day trading. He failed, but in doing so, learnt a lot. To find out more, visit Maitland's Web site (www.howtomake yourmillion.com).

For a more exhaustive approach on share trading, I recommend *Trading for a Living*, by Dr Alexander Elder (John Wiley, 1993). Most books on trading are dully written, but this one is intriguing. It places emphasis on trader psychology, and technical analysis. A study guide with multiple choice questions is separately available.

If you are considering day trading in the US market, read *Day Trade Online*, by Christopher Farrell (John Wiley, 1999). This book is strong on how to exploit the bid–ask spread on share price quotes. For the views of successful US traders, read *Stock Market Wizards*, by Jack D Schwager (John Wiley, 2001), who also wrote the acclaimed classic *Market Wizards*.

Do not miss *Reminiscences of a Stock Operator*, by Edwin Lefevre (John Wiley, 1994). The book, which is compulsory reading for novices on some City and Wall Street trading floors, is a thinly disguised account of the life of legendary share trader Jesse Livermore. It shows how, as a trader, you should not fight the market.

Also read *The Disciplined Trader: Developing winning attitudes*, by Mark Douglas (New York Institute of Finance, 1990). This book is a riveting study of the psychology of trading. The author argues that, to trade successfully, you must develop new perspectives without boundaries. As reviews on bookshop Web sites show, many readers praise the book wholeheartedly, while a few dismiss it as new age nonsense. To find out more, visit the author's Web site at www.markdouglas.com.

Technical analysis

If you are interested in technical analysis, read the classic primer *Charters on Charting* (Batsford Business Books, 1995). This simplified introduction has got many enthusiasts started. The author has taken a chatty approach, citing his personal experience. There is nothing to touch this book for readability. I also recommend Martin Pring's introduction to *Technical Analysis* (McGraw-Hill, 1999), which has a useful CD ROM with it.

If you are ready for a more comprehensive approach, go for *Technical Analysis Explained* by Martin J Pring (McGraw-Hill, 1991), which is highly readable. For a more old-fashioned approach, read *Technical Analysis of Stock Trends* by Robert D Edwards and John Magee, (New York Institute of Finance, 1992). The text is clear, thorough and authoritative, although it can seem laboured.

To see how a master investor uses technical analysis, read *Winning on Wall Street* by Martin Zweig (Warner Books, 1994). The author, one of the great US stock pickers, reveals his favourite technical indicators, and how to get the best from them.

I would also recommend *How to Make Money in Stocks* by William O'Neil (McGraw-Hill, 1995). The author, a master investor, offers a proven stock market investing system which relies partly on technical analysis.

Spread betting

If you want to read about spread betting, avoid the over-priced, self-published manuals on the subject that are available by mail order. Instead, buy *Market Speculating* by Andrew Burke (Rowton Press, 1999). This readable short guide covers the pros and cons of spread betting, and how to work the system to your best advantage. It has informative sections on trading tactics, and on technical analysis.

For a perspective on short selling, which you may do through spread betting, read *Profit of the Plunge* by Simon Cawkwell (Rushmere Wynne, 1995). This is a confessional and how-to book rolled into one by the legendary short seller whom the press has dubbed Evil Knievel.

Derivatives

In books on options, simplicity is a virtue. For the basics, try *Understand Derivatives in a Day* (Take That, 1995), or *Investing in Traded Options* by Robert Linggard (Take That, 2000). To read how professionals can manipulate derivatives and come unstuck, read *Rogue Trader* by Nick Leeson (Warner Books, 1999). The author is the disgraced trader who brought down Barings, the merchant bank.

Making sense of a company report and accounts

If you know nothing about understanding a company report and accounts, you will obtain a clear overview from *Understanding Company Financial Statements* by R H Parker (Penguin Business, 1988). The book focuses on analysis and interpretation rather than practical accounting techniques.

For more ambitious readers, the bible on the subject remains *Interpreting Company Reports and Accounts* by Geoffrey Holmes and Alan Sugden (Prentice Hall Woodhead-Faulkner, Seventh Edition). This is a very readable reference book. For advanced readers, a useful companion volume is *Beyond the Balance Sheet*, by Geoffrey Holmes and Robin Dunham (Woodhead-Faulkner, 1994).

For an approach that is more like a course, try *The Motley Fool UK Investment Workbook*, by David Berger and Bruce Jackson (Boxtree, 1999). The authors offer an unconventional but accessible approach hallmarked by the usual Motley Fool facetiousness.

Although it is now a few years old, *Accounting for Growth: Stripping the camouflage from company accounts*, by Terry Smith (Century Business, 1996) makes eye-opening reading for novices. It demonstrates how named quoted companies have used creative accounting. When it was first published, the book was an immediate bestseller, which was unheard of for a book on accounting.

Value investing and ratio analysis

To see how value investing works in practice, try *John Neff on Investing* (John Wiley, 1999). The book explains how John Neff, a master US fund manager, beat the market in 22 years out of 31 as portfolio manager for Vanguard's Windsor and Gemini Funds. Also read *Security Analysis on Wall Street*, by Jeffrey C Hooke (John Wiley, 1998). It usefully covers modern techniques of equity analysis used on Wall Street.

To get to grips with the investment techniques of Warren Buffett, the most successful value investor in history, read *Buffettology*, by Mary Buffett and David Clark (Pocket Books, 1999). The book clearly describes his investment methods, including the annual compounding rate of return. On Buffett's broader thinking, try *Warren Buffett Speaks*, compiled by Janet Lowe (John Wiley, 1997). This is a well organized compendium of quotations from the master.

Growth investing

To learn more about growth investing, try Jim Slater's books. They are fascinating and highly readable. *The Zulu Principle* (Orion, 1993) is perhaps his masterpiece. But do not read uncritically as Slater's approach, convincing as it may sound, does not always work.

Also, read *Investing Common Stocks and Uncommon Profits*, by Philip A Fisher (John Wiley, 1996). This classic, written by a master investor, has influenced none less than Warren Buffett. The book focuses on qualitative rather than quantitative stock selection criteria for long-term growth investing.

A reviewer on the Web site of bookseller Amazon commented aptly:

> From reading Fisher, I now understand that one should only invest in a small number of stocks, but these stocks must be perfect in all aspects. He shows one what signs to look for in a company and how to analyse it. From reading Mr Fisher's book, I have put all my money in Coca Cola, and have been well rewarded.

Discounted Cash Flow (DCF) analysis

Arguably the most accessible book on DCF analysis is *The Penguin Guide to Finance* (Penguin Books, 2000). This is entertainingly presented, and favours back-of-the-envelope calculations over complex spreadsheet work. The author is Hugo Dixon, who used to run the Lex column in the *Financial Times*. Also visit his Web site Breakingviews (www.breakingviews.com), which provides an intelligent critical perspective on financial news.

Also useful is *Introduction to Corporate Finance, Workbook 8*, edited by DC Gardner (FT Pitman Publishing, 1996). This workbook sets out a clear step-by-step introduction to corporate finance, including explanations of DCF analysis and the Capital Asset Pricing Model.

Internet and other high-tech stocks

Books on valuing high-tech stocks, like some of the technology they cover, become outdated. Some are also more accessible to the layman than others. Let me tell you about the most readable basic guide to investing in high-tech stocks that I have ever come across. This is *The Big Tech Score* by Mike Kwatinetz, with Danielle Kwatinetz Wood (John Wiley, 2001). This book has two major qualities. First, the main author is a leading Wall Street investment analyst, so he knows what he is talking about. Second, the style is exceptionally easy to read. Try it.

You should also read *Super Stocks*, by Kenneth Fisher (IRWIN Professional Publishing, 1984). This pioneering classic shows you how to use the price/sales ratio and the price/research ratio to select bargain-basement high-tech stocks.

For an overview, you could do worse than read *The Secrets of Investing in Technology Stocks*, by Edward Trapunski (John Wiley, 1998). Although the book has too fragmented an approach, it offers useful ground rules and insights.

Economics

The most readable guide to interpreting economic statistics that I have ever come across is *Market Movers* by Nancy Dunnan and Jay J Pick (Warner Books, 1993). The authors explain how you should adjust your investment strategies to match economic statistics, trends and news events. It is annoying that this excellent book focuses only on the US economy.

A survival guide to UK economic indicators and how to interpret them is *The Economist Guide to Economic Indicators* (*The Economist* in conjunction with Profile Books, 1997). An alternative book, which I find less readable, is *The Financial Times Guide to Using Economics and Economic Indicators*, by Romesh Vaitilingham (Financial Times Pitman Publishing, 1994).

On how economic statistics are manipulated, I recommend *How to Lie With Statistics*, by Darrell Huff (Penguin, 1991). This light classic will amuse as well as inform you. For a more thorough approach, try *Measuring the Economy, A guide to understanding official statistics*, by Christopher Johnson and Simon Briscoe (Penguin, 1995).

Sharp practice and fraud

There are surprisingly few books advising you on how to detect and protect yourself against the tricks of the dubious stockbroker or financial adviser. This is partly due to libel risk, but also due to ignorance. A readable book from the United States that covers this and related areas is *Fraud! How to Protect Yourself From Schemes, Scams and Swindles*, by Marsha Bertrand (AMACOM, 1999).

You can still obtain copies of my first book *The City Share Pushers* (Scope Books, 1989), which is about sharp practice among City-of-London share dealers. The firms that I exposed no longer exist, but stockbrokers still use the dubious stock promotion techniques described.

Some books by one time stock market guru Robert Beckman touch on financial fraud. In his ambitious *Into the Upwave* (Milestone Publications, 1988), he suggests that sharp practice is rife in the City of London. Here is an extract:

> The City, which is synonymous with the nationwide securities industry, is full of special types, nearly all of whom are arrogant. Some of them are very rich; and some of them, according to the rules the average citizen obeys, are very crooked. Behind the gleaming smiles, the pin-striped suits, the school ties and the red carnation lies very often an inner contempt for the average investor.

Broaden your reading horizons

Let me tell you about a rather oddball book that you may find interesting. It is *Bears & Bulls: The psychology of the stock market* by

David Cohen (Metro, 2000). The author is a psychologist and journalist, and his book offers fascinating views on the deeper motivation of stockbrokers.

In addition, it is worth understanding how professional fund managers select stocks and manage portfolios as, in doing so, they wield enormous influence over share prices. For this, read *The City: Inside the great expectation machine*, by Tony Golding (Financial Times Prentice Hall, 2001). For more detail on how fund managers, and analysts, select stocks, read *The Super Analysts*, by Andrew Leeming (John Wiley, 2000). The book contains candid interviews with top performers.

On the case for getting your money out of equities, read *Valuing Wall Street* by Andrew Smithers and Stephen Wright (McGraw Hill, 2000). The book presents a compelling theory on how today's stock markets are overvalued. Its case is based on Nobel Laureate James Tobin's 'q' concept.

If you want to read about unconventional tax avoidance techniques, offshore investment, and related areas from a UK perspective, an easy-to-read beginners' guide is *Privacy* by Stuart Goldsmith (Medina, 1997). The author also publishes a related subscription-only newsletter. Visit his Web site at www.stuartgoldsmith.com.

Financial fiction

You can learn about the financial world from good relevant novels more painlessly than from non-fiction. But you need to read an author that suits you. For instance, some investors enjoy the financial thrillers of ex-bond trader Michael Ridpath, but I do not.

I have had a couple of financial novels published myself. You will enjoy these if you like to learn about the wilder side of the stock market by losing yourself in a story. My latest is *Stock Market Rollercoaster* (John Wiley, 2001) and it tells of a green young man's hair-raising apprenticeship to a master stock market trader. At the risk of blowing my own trumpet, I believe that my book will tell you more about the stock market than you will get out of reading most non-fiction books. My earlier novel, that went into a second print run, was *The Survivors* (Scope Books, 1990), a story of stockbroking fraud.

A gripping financial thriller, in my view, is *The Watchmen* by Matthew Lynn (Arrow Books, 1999). It tells of a former stockbroking analyst and an employee of the Serious Fraud Office who becomes a fugitive after he has stumbled on an insider-dealing ring. The story puts the relationship between analysts, the press and quoted companies under the spotlight.

Amusingly, the author tried to promote *The Watchmen* on the Motley Fool UK Web site through the message boards, offering the first chapter free to any interested party. This was how I first became alerted to the book's existence. Then users of the message boards objected to this unorthodox publicity gambit, and Lynn backed off.

Another novel which throws light on how the City works is *Trixie Trader*, written by *Daily Telegraph* financial journalist Helen Dunne. Written with gentle humour, this offers insight into deal-making behind the scenes in the City.

If you are thinking of investing in emerging markets, try reading fiction related to the countries in question. For a perspective on Russia experienced at first hand by the author, I recommend *Slaphead*, by Georgina Wroe (Headline, 1999).

The way forward

Books cannot replace investment experience, but can supplement it. It is no wonder that online investors build their own small library, and regularly keep an eye on new titles published. If this module inspires you to do the same, it will have achieved its objective.

Dynamic rules of the Online Share Buyer's FlexiSystem

- Read investment books to supplement your practical investing experience, but not to replace it.
- Before you buy an investment book, read any reviews published online.
- Read relevant fiction as well as non-fiction.

A final word

Congratulations on finishing this book. It is a sign of your real interest in online investing that you have got this far.

If you have the commitment and the guts for this business, do not linger too long on fantasy trading. As we have seen, it does not replicate the stomach-churning ups and downs that you feel when you put real money on the line.

There is only one way forward now and that is through real online investing experience. You must open up a broking account, if you have not done so already, and start dealing in shares, putting the knowledge you have gained into practice.

Set aside some initial capital that you can afford to lose, take a deep breath and build – slowly and carefully – a real portfolio. Initially five shares with £1,000–£2,000 in each one would be a good starting point. But you do not have to buy them all at once.

You can never find out enough about the companies and sectors in which you are invested, or are planning to invest. Keep reading and researching. If in the immediate future you want a primer beyond this one, the London *Evening Standard* has been kind enough to recommend my best-selling book *How to Win in a Volatile Stock Market* (Kogan Page, 2000) for share traders. The book describes a successful method of value investing and usefully complements the coverage in these pages. If you buy a copy, it will amply repay the investment.

Also consider subscribing to *Secrets of Growing Rich: The complete investment mastery course*. This explains in simple language how to make money on the stock market. I have contributed myself to this course and am confident that you will find it helpful. For details, contact Fleet Street Letter Publications (www.sgrhelpdesk@f-s-p.co.uk).

Otherwise, do not neglect conventional seminars and courses, as well as, of course, the financial press. Beyond this, the Internet is the most bountiful source of ongoing global financial information and news available.

Soon you will find that you are part of a global community of investors. You can speak to others through the Internet chat rooms. You can find out the latest thinking on day trading in the United States through the many relevant Web sites.

Online, you can track your portfolio and obtain real time share prices. This gives you every incentive to take an orderly approach. Keep your contract notes and share certificates carefully. Also keep a note of any important conversations with your broker, complete with time and date. You should record share price and index changes regularly. This way, you can later review how the Online Share Buyer's FlexiSystem is working for you.

From this book, you will have gained an excellent grounding. *But it will only have truly succeeded in its mission when you have reached the stage when you can let the book go, kick away the crutches, and make your own investment decisions.* It is then that you will truly join the small band of successful online investors who do it our way.

We are technically at the end of the course, but all is not over. I would love to hear from you directly. Do get in touch with comments, queries, or suggestions for improving this book in the next edition. Drop me a line via the publisher, or directly at alexander davidson@lineone.net. Alternatively, visit my Web site at www.flexinvest.co.uk. In the meantime, I wish you an enjoyable and, above all, *lucrative* experience of online investing.

Appendix

Useful Web sites

Here is my own selection of useful Web sites. As seasoned users of the Internet know, one site leads into another, and the range is always changing. Use these Web sites as your starting point, and develop your own list.

General

Flexinvest – this is the author's own Web site. Visit me there as soon as possible at www.flexinvest.co.uk. I explain many amazingly useful investment techniques on this site, and the best thing is that it's all free. Do not miss it. Also, I welcome your comments or queries about this book, or any aspect of the stock market via the site.

Hemmington Scott – arguably the best source of free information on UK quoted companies, including a five year summary profit and loss account with balance sheet, share price movements, major shareholders and similar:
www.hemscott.com/equities

itruffle – a lively investor resource for the small cap sector:
www.itruffle.com

MoneyExtra – introduction to the stock market, and share tracking:
www.moneyextra.com

Mrscohen.co.uk – A lively basic Web site on the stock market and personal finance, run by author and broadcaster **Bernice Cohen**:
www.mrscohen.co.uk

Wright Research Center – key ratios and price trend analysis, latest earnings and dividends and much more on 18,000 companies worldwide:
http://www.profiles.wisi.com/

Favourite general stock market Web sites

Ample
www.ample.com

The Motley Fool UK
www.fool.co.uk

Favourite search engines

www.yahoo.com

www.google.com

www.excite.com

Exchanges

London Stock Exchange – a highly informative and useful Web site:
www.londonstockexchange.com

NASDAQ – the US high-tech market:
www.nasdaq.co.uk

Share price quotes

Freequotes
www.freequotes.co.uk)

Londonmoneymarket.com – live share prices, charts, quotes and ticker:
www.londonmoneymarket.com

Marketeye – various services for price quotes and data, accessed through www.thomsonfn.com:
www.marketeye.co.uk

Teletext
www.teletext.co.uk

Wall Street City – real-time US quotes:
www.wallstreetcity.com

Setting up an online portfolio

Ample
www.ample.com

Stock screeners

Hoovers
www.hoovers.com

Marketeye
www.marketeye.co.uk – accessed through www.thomsonfn.com

MarketGuide
www.marketguide.com

MarketPlayer.com
www.marketplayer.com/scrn/

Quicken.com
www.quicken.com/investments/stocks

Yahoo
http://screen.yahoo.com/stocks.html

Selecting your stockbroker

The Association of Private Client Investment Managers and Stockbrokers – a list of brokers (online and otherwise): www.apcims.co.uk

Money extra – online brokers compared: www.moneyextra.com

Comparison of brokers

www.gomez.com (click into the UK section)

Motley Fool UK – a table comparing costs of online brokers, and related message boards: www.fool.co.uk

Online stockbrokers

Abbey National Sharedealing Service
e-mail: Nick.crabb@abbeynational.co.uk

Barclays Stockbrokers
www.barclays-stockbrokers.co.uk

James Brearley & Sons
www.jbrearley.co.uk

Cave & Sons Limited
www.caves.co.uk

Charles Schwab
e-mail: webinquiries@schwab-europe.com

Charles Stanley
www.charles.stanley.co.uk

City Deal Services
e-mail: shares@citydeal.co.uk

comdirect
e-mail: info@comdirect.co.uk

Davy Stockbrockers
www.davy.ie

DLJ Direct
www.dljdirect.co.uk

Durlacher Ltd
www.durlacher.com

e-cortal
www.e-cortal.com

egg
www.egg.com

E*Trade
www.etrade.co.uk

Fastrade
www.fastrade.co.uk

Goy Harris Cartwright
www.ghcl.co.uk

Halifax ShareXpress
www.sharexpress.co.uk

Hargreaves Landsdown
www.h-l.co.uk

Killik & Co
www.killik.co.uk

Murray Beith Murray Asset Management
e-mail: asset@murraybeith.co.uk

MyBroker (active trader broker)
www.mybroker.co.uk

NatWest Stockbrokers
www.natweststockbrokers.co.uk

Redmayne Bentley (REDM – Online Trading)
www.redm.co.uk

Self Trade UK Ltd
e-mail: info@self-trade.co.uk

The Share Centre
www.share.co.uk

Share People
e-mail: info@sharepeople.com

Stock Academy
www.stockacademy.com

Stocktrade
www.stocktrade.co.uk

Teather & Greenwood
www.teathers.com

Torrie & Co
www.torrie.co.uk

Virgin Money
www.virginmoney.com

Walker, Crips, Weddle and Beck
e-mail: clientservices@wcwb.co.uk

TD Waterhouse
www.tdwaterhouse.co.uk

Xest
www.xest.com

How spread betting works

Onewaybet.com – my favourite Web site about spread betting:
www.onewaybet.com

The Internet Sporting Club
www.internetsportingclub.co.uk

spreadbetting explained
www.spreadbettingexplained.com

spreadbets.net
www.spreadbets.net

Spread betting firms

Cantor Index
www.cantorindex.com

City Index
www.cityindex.co.uk

Financial Spreads
www.finspreads.com

IG Index
www.igindex.co.uk

Spreadex
www.spreadex.co.uk

How CFDs work

Copperchip
www.copperchip.co.uk

IGIndex Direct
www.igshares.com

Sucden UK
www.equitycfd.co.uk

CFD dealers

UK

Cantor Index
www.cantorindexcfd.com

City Markets
www.citymarkets.net

Client2Client
www.client2client.com

Deal4free
www.cmcplc.com/shares

GNI Touch
www.gni.co.uk

Halewood International Futures
www.hifutures.com

IFX
www.ifx.co.uk

IG Markets
www.igshares.com

ManDirect
www.mandirect.co.uk

Sucden Equities CFDs
www.equitycfd.co.uk

US

Carlin
www.carlingroup.com

CyBerCorp
www.cybertrader.com

Interactive Brokers
www.interactivebrokers.com

Tradecast
www.tradecast.com

Forex trading firms

Cantor Fitzgerald International
www.cantor.com

DigitalLook – comprehensive directory of forex dealing firms:
www.digitallook.com

ED&F Man
www.edfman.com

GNI
www.gni.co.uk

Lind-Waldock (a US firm)
www.lind-waldock.com

Sucden
www.sucden.co.uk

Forex news and research

Forexia – news and research on the forex markets:
www.gen-fx.com/forexia.htm

Trend Analysis – an independent service offering reports on currency movements:
www.trend-analysis.com

Discount brokers (financial services)

Acumen Investments – includes discount service:
www.acumen-investments.com

Aisa direct
www.aisa.co.uk

Alder Broker Group
www.abgltd.co.uk

Bestinvest
www.bestinvest.co.uk

Chartwell
www.chartwell-investment.co.uk

Cheapfunds.co.uk
www.cheapfunds.co.uk

Chelsea Financial Services
www.chelseafs.co.uk

Direct investor
www.direct-investor.com

Discount Investments Ltd
www.discount-investments.co.uk

Facet Direct
www.facet-ifa.com

Garrison Investment Analysis
www.garrison.co.uk

Hargreaves Lansdown
www.hargreaveslansdown.co.uk

Heritage Financial Services
www.heritage-financial.co.uk

Investment Discount House
www.idh.co.uk

Investment Discounts On-Line UK
www.theidol.co.uk

ISAVED
www.isaved.co.uk

Max Value
www.maxvalue.co.uk

Moneyworld-ifa
www.moneyworld-ifa.co.uk

PEP-TopTen.com
www.pep-topten.com

quickdiscounts.com
www.quickdiscounts.com

Seymour Sinclair Investments
www.seymoursinclair.co.uk

Analysts' research

Institutional Investor – list of top analysts and their track record:
www.iimagazine.com

General

FirstCall Research Direct
www.firstcall.com

Multex Investor
www.multexinvestor.com

Thomson Financial Web site
www.thomsoninvest.net

Specific

Analyst – detailed financial analysis for private investors:
www.analystinvestor.com

Beeson Gregory – small- and medium-sized companies in Europe:
www.beeson-gregory.co.uk

Charles Schwab – US-based analyst centre:
www.schwab.com

DLJ Direct (also gives access to US bureau services including Zack's company report, and S&P MarketScope):
www.dljdirect.com

Equity Development – analysts' reports commissioned by companies:
www.equity-development.co.uk

Equityinvestigator – independent analysts' research on high-tech stocks:
www.equityinvestigator.com

IDEAGLobal – former investment bank analysts' independent research covering US markets:
www.ideaglobal.com

Merrill Lynch HSBC – good free investment research:
www.mlhsbc.com

Moneyguru (own analysts)
www.moneyguru.com

Peel Hunt – for small subscription, research and video interviews:
www.peelhunt.com

Salomon Smith Barney
www.salomonsmithbarney.com

SG Cowen – technology-driven investment bank:
www.sgcowen.com

UBS Warburg
www.ubsw.com

Analysts' consensus ratings

Hemscott
www.hemscott.net

Sharescope.com
www.sharescope.com

Stock market news

Bloomberg
www.bloomberg.co.uk

DigitalLook – news alerts by e-mail on a trader's portfolio of stocks:
www.digitallook.com

Electronic Telegraph
www.telegraph.co.uk

Evening Standard online
www.thisislondon.com

The Financial Times
www.ft.com

Fleet Street Publications – Britain's largest investment newsletter publisher:
www.fleetstreetpublications.co.uk

Forbes – US business magazine:
www.forbes.com

Guardian Unlimited
www.guardian.co.uk

Investors Chronicle
www.investorschronicle.co.uk

The Motley Fool UK
www.fool.co.uk

The Motley Fool US
www.fool.com

News review – a summary of the weekend City press:
www.news-review.co.uk

Newsletter Publishing – how to subscribe to The AIM Newsletter (and sister publications). Sample copies provided online:
www.redskyresearch.com

Red Herring magazine – high-tech developments in the United States:
www.redherring.com

This Is Money – news archives of *The Daily Mail, Mail on Sunday,* and *Evening Standard*:
www.thisismoney.co.uk

Times-Money
www.times-money.co.uk

Tipsheets.co.uk – details of leading tipsheets on the market:
www.tipsheets.co.uk

Share traders

Career DayTrader.com – useful articles and interviews related to day trading:
www.careerdaytrader.com

Cyberinvest – information and links for home-based traders:
www.cyberinvest.com

DayTraders.com
www.daytraders.com

Jonathan Maitland, a journalist, records his own share trading experiences:
www.howtomakeyourmillion.com

Robert Miner's Web site – useful advice on trading:
www.dynamictraders.com

Information/prices on options, warrants and futures

Chicago Board of Traded Options Exchange
www.cboe.com

The London International Financial Futures and Options Exchange (LIFFE)
www.liffe.com

Marketeye – derivatives exchange information included:
www.marketeye.co.uk – accessed through www.thomsonfn.com

Shaeffersresearch.com – an overview on options and how they work:
www.shaeffersresearch.com

Warrants Alert – a newsletter on warrants and an introductory guide:
www.tipsheets.co.uk

Options and futures dealers

Berkeley Futures
www.bfl.co.uk

Easy2Trade
www.easy2trade.com

Futures-investor.com
www.futures-investor.co.uk

GNI
www.gni.com

Halewood International Futures
www.hifutures.com

ManDirect
www.mandirect.co.uk

Options Direct
www.mybroker.co.uk

Technical analysis

Ample – another useful chart search facility:
www.ample.com

DecisionPoint.com – material on charting, some free, the rest for subscribers only:
www.decisionpoint.com

Digitallook – giving access to charts:
www.digitallook.com

FTMarketWatch – offering an excellent charting facility:
www.ftmarketwatch.com

murphymorris.com – leading market technician John Murphy addresses subscribers:
www.murphymorris.com

mytrack program – if you want to draw your own trend lines
www.mytrack.com

StockCharts.com – an excellent general site on charting:
www.stockcharts.com

Technical analysis from A to Z – highly informative:
www.equis.com/free/taaz

Professional charting programmes

Indexia
www.indexia.co.uk

Omnitrader
www.omnitrader.com

Synergy
www.synergy.com

Updata
www.updata.com

Services offering an anonymous e-mail address

The following sites can be used to set up an anonymous e-mail address (for research without risking being deluged with spam mail).

Bigfoot
www.bigfoot.com

Hotmail
www.hotmail.com

Yahoo
www.yahoo.com

Company research

Corporate reports
www.corpreports.co.uk

Dr Ed Yardeni's Economics Network – US economics and stock market research from the chief global economist of Deutsche Bank

Securities in New York:
www.yardeni.com

FinancialWeb – US news, research, Securities & Exchange Commission filings, and company reports:
www.financialweb.com

Hemscott.net
www.hemscott.net

Hoover's Online – online details of more than 15,000 companies worldwide:
www.hoovers.com

Investor-relations
www.investor-relations.co.uk

Zacks.com – brokers' reports and news (US site):
www.zacks.com

Penny Shares

Use these sites for background information and perspectives. If you want to buy, I advise you to do your own research.

Ameritech – Penny Stock Portal:
www.ameritech.net

City Equities – UK penny share dealer:
www.cityequities.com

Penny Investor.com
www.pennyinvestor.com

Penny Shares Ltd.com – an online tipsheet:
www.pennysharesltd.com

Pennystockinsider.com
www.pennystockinsider.com

Penny Stocks.net – advice on US pink sheets stocks:
www.penny-stocks.net

Rollercoaster Stocks
www.rollercoasterstocks.com

High-tech stocks

Durlacher, the investment boutique:
www.durlacher.com

Richard Holway Ltd
www.holway.com

Silicon Investor
www.techstocks.com

WitCapital, the online investment bank:
www.witcapital.com

Internet message boards

The Motley Fool UK
www.fool.co.uk

The Motley Fool US
www.fool.com

Raging Bull
www.ragingbull.com

Silicon Investor – subscription-based but high quality:
www.techstocks.com

Yahoo
finance.yahoo.com

Web page providing links to message boards of Market Eye, Hemmington Scott, UK Shares and Interactive Investor:
www.freeyellow.com/members6/scottit/page7.html

Digitallook.com – bulletin board comments round-up:
www.digitallook.com

Investment courses/educational

Investor's Business Daily – free course online (including technical analysis) from US guru William O'Neil:
www.investors.com

Martin Cole's four-day futures trading course on the Costa del Sol:
www.learningtotrade.com

Sharecrazy.com
www.sharecrazy.com

Stock Academy – general stock market education:
www.stockacademy.com

Success Investor training:
www.success-events.com

The Siroc site – educational on futures and options:
www.siroc.co.uk

Tradebasic.com – an educational service for investors
www.tradebasics.com

Fantasy trading

DLJdirect – excellent demo:
www.dljdirect.co.uk

Hollywood Stock Exchange – fantasy trading in film stars and musicians as practice for stock market trading:
www.hsx.com

Selftrade – excellent demo trading:
www.selftrade.com

Tax

Ample – UK taxes explained, news of tax efficient investments, help with tax returns, online discussion group:
www.ample.com/tax

Blythens – tax advice:
www.blythens.co.uk

Deloitte & Touche – tax advice:
www.deloitte.co.uk

Inland Revenue
www.inlandrevenue.gov.uk

Money World Web site – inheritance tax page:
www.moneyworld.co.uk/glossary/gl00149.htm

Details of tax rates:
www.glazers.co.uk

OFEX

Equities Direct – online broker dealing in OFEX stocks:
www.equities-direct.co.uk

OFEX Web site:
www.ofex.com

unquoted.co.uk – news, information, interviews and message boards on OFEX companies:
www.unquoted.co.uk

AIM

BDO Stoy Hayward – accountancy firm specializing in AIM:
www.bdo.co.uk

Graham H Wills & Company – a stockbroker that offers IPOs in OFEX and AIM stocks:
www.ghw.co.uk

Newsletter Publishing Ltd – relevant tip sheets:
www.redsky.com

TechMARK

The London Stock Exchange
www.londonstockexchange.com/techmark

Directors' dealings

Citywire
www.citywire.co.uk

Digitallook
www.digitallook.com

UK-invest
www.uk-invest.co.uk

International investing

Dover Capital – useful on investing in Russia:
www.dover-capital.com

Japanese company financial statements – English language version:
japanfinancials.com

JP Morgan's ADR Web site – useful on ADRs:
www.adr.com

Foreign stock exchanges

Athens Stock Exchange
www.ase.gr

Australian Stock Exchange (ASX)
www.asx.com.au/

BorsaOnWeb – Italian stock prices:
www.telematica.it/borsaOnWeb.html

Caracas Stock Exchange, Venezuela
www.caracasstock.com/english.htm

Deutsche Borse, Germany
www.exchange.de/

Geneva Stock Exchange, Switzerland
www.bourse.ch/

Johannesburg Stock Exchange, South Africa
www.jse.co.za/

Lisbon Stock Exchange, Portugal
www.bvl.pt/

Madrid Stock Exchange
www.bolsamadrid.es/

Montreal Exchange
www.me.org/

Nasdaq – US high-tech market:
www.nasdaq.com/

National Stock Exchange of India
www.nseindia.com/

New York Stock Exchange
www.nyse.com

Paris Stock Exchange
www.bourse-de-paris.fr/

Stock Exchange of Singapore
www.ses.com.sg/

Stockholm Stock Exchange, Sweden
www.stockholmborsen.se

Tel-Aviv Stock Exchange, Israel
www.tase.co.il/

The Prague Stock Exchange (details)
www.pse.cz

The Stock Exchange of Thailand
www.set.or.th/

Vancouver Stock Exchange – this has merged with the Alberta Exchange to form the Canadian Venture Exchange:
www.cdnx.com

Zagreb Stock Exchange, Croatia
www.zse.com.hr

Free samples of financial newsletters

www.financial-freebies.com

www.thefreestuffgallery.com

Unconventional financial advice

Eden Press – leading California-based seller of unconventional tax haven books:
www.edenpress.com

The offshore secrets network – a glimpse into unconventional offshore investing:
www.offshoresecrets.com

The Sovereign Society – unconventional tax haven advice:
www.sovereignsociety.com

Stuart Goldsmith – seller of privacy-type information:
www.stuartgoldsmith.com

WAP Sites

Ample – general financial Web site:
www.ample.co.uk

Financial Times
wap.ft.com

London Stock Exchange – market news and other information:
wap.priceinhand.com

Mobile Invest
www.mobile-invest.co.uk

moneyeXtra – stock quotes, charts, portfolio tracking, and financial data:
wap.moneyextra.com

Stock Smart – access to US stock portfolio:
wap.stocksmart.com

TD Waterhouse – a broker site:
wap.tdwaterhouse.co.uk

Complaints

The Financial Services Authority
www.fsa.gov.uk

The Securities & Futures Association
www.sfa.org.uk

Investment clubs

Proshare
www.proshare.org

New issues

Financial News – another leading publication about new issues on capital markets:
www.efinancialnews.com

Issues direct – a Web site specializing in new issues:
www.issuesdirect.com

International Financing Review – the market leader about new issues on capital markets:
www.ifrweb.com

UK-iNvest.com – useful coverage of new issues:
www.uk-invest.co.uk

Books

Amazon – cut-price books and online reviews:
www.amazon.co.uk

Books.co.uk – price surveys and other comparisons of online bookshops:
www.books.co.uk

Global-investor – an excellent large online bookshop:
www.global-investor.com

Index

abroad *see* international investing
accounting tricks *see* creative accounting
accounts, company 9, 39–41, 176
accounts, opening online 28
acid test 44
active trader brokers 21–22, 64
ADRs (American depositary receipts) 17
advance revenue recognition 97
advisory brokers 22, 159–70
   dubious tricks 161–69
   selecting 160–61
AIM (Alternative Investment Market) 99–100, 113
   Web sites 100, 204–05
American depositary receipts (ADRs) 17
Ameritrade 26
Ample 14
analyst 127
analysts 10–11, 53–55, 115
   Web sites 194–96
analytical techniques 37–57
   Internet companies 49–51
   macro-economic factors 51–55
   qualitative factors 48–49
   value and growth investing 38–48
annual reports and accounts 39–41, 176
anonymous e-mail addresses, sites offering 200
arbitrage 151
asset backing, and penny share trading 96
assets, fixed and current 40
'at the money' 135
auditor's reports 39
average earnings index, as inflationary indicator 52

back-up services, brokers' 23
balance sheets 39, 40
Bank of England 51
banks, new issue involvement 116–17
bar charts 76
Bargain Hunters' Investment FlexiSystem 5
Barings Bank collapse 139–40
bearish strategies on options 138
beginners' Web sites 13–14
Berger, David 129
'beta' figures 48
'better technology spiral' trick 164–65
biotechnology companies 94
Black-Scholes model 141
Bollinger bands 85
bonus issues 31–32
bookbuilding periods 112
bookmakers, choosing financial 151–52
bookrunners 110
bookshops, online 171–72, 209
'break forwards' 138
brokers, online 3–4, 5–6, 8, 19–31, 35–36
   advisory compared 159–69
   CFD dealing 155
   checklist 23–27
   comparisons 27
   dealing mechanics 27–31
   options 142
   reasons for using 19–23
   share trading 64
   useful Web sites 187–89, 192–94
browser-based brokers 21, 64
bucket shops 166
Buffett, Warren 9, 127, 177

bullish strategies on options 137–38
business-to-consumer Internet companies 50
'butterflies' 139

Call options 134–35, 137–38
candlestick charts 77–78
Capital Asset Pricing Model (CAPM) 48
capital gains tax (CGT) 104
capitalized expenses 96
capitalization issues 31–32
CAPM (Capital Asset Pricing Model) 48
capped options 134
Carphone Warehouse 118–19
cash flow 9, 46–48
'cash flow per share' ratio 46
cash-flow statements 39, 40–41
CFDs 153–55
　Web sites 155, 190–92
CGT (capital gains tax) 104
chairman's statements 39
Chart Prophet, The 87
charts, technical analysis 76–83
　patterns 81–83
　plotting and using 78–81
circles of competence 10
clubs, investment 12–13, 208
Cole, Martin 69
company accounts 9, 39–41, 176
company research Web sites 200–01
compensation scheme 34
complaints 33–34
　Web sites 208
computer upgrades 28
'concealed churn' trick 164
'condors' 139
consensus forecasts 55, 196
continuation patterns 81–82
contrarian investing, tip sheet coverage 127
Coppock indicator 85
costs of dealing 24
courses
　hands-on trading 69
　online 15, 203
'covering-up ignorance' trick 165–66
creative accounting 41–42, 96–97
Crest computerized system 30
Crest-sponsored member accounts 30
current assets and liabilities 40
current ratio 44

cyclical stocks 93

day trading 60, 174
day trading centres 63
DCF *see* discounted cash flow analysis
'dead cross' signs 84
dealing costs 24
dealing mechanics 27–30
decision trees 50
directors' dealings Web sites 205
discount brokers 6, 192–94
discounted cash-flow (DCF) analysis 9, 47
　recommended reading 177–78
discount rates 47
discretionary accounts 159–60
'disguised churn' trick 164
diversification 11–12
dividend cover 44
dividends 31, 43–44
'double top or bottom' reversal pattern 83
Dow Theory 75–76
dual trading 154
dubious dealers *see* unscrupulous dealers
'dubious stock promotions' trick 166–67

earnings before interest and tax (EBIT) 47
earnings before interest, tax, depreciation and amortization (EBITDA) ratio 45
earnings per share (eps) ratio 41–42
EBIT (earnings before interest and tax) 47
EBITDA (earnings before interest, tax, depreciation and amortization)
　ratio 45
economics, recommended reading 178–79
education, online investment 15, 205
efficient market hypothesis 5
Egyptian ratchet 139
EIS (Enterprise Investment Scheme) 103–04
Elliot Wave theory 87
e-mail addresses, services offering anonymous 200
'e-mail service' brokers 20–21
emerging markets 16–17
encryption 24
Enterprise Investment Scheme (EIS) 103–04
enterprise value 45
'envelopes' 84–85
EPIC code 28
eps (earnings per share) 41–42

Index 213

Equities Direct service 99
equivolume charts 78
European-style options 134
exchange rates 16, 26
execution-only brokers 5, 19–20

failures by share traders 61–62
fan lines 80
fantasy (simulated) trading 25, 70
   Web sites 203
favoured sector new issues 118
Fibonacci ratios 86–87
fiction, financial 180–81
financial fiction 180–81
financial futures 147–48
   spread betting 148–53
   Web sites 198–99
financial news Web sites 26, 63–64, 196–97
Financial Services Authority (FSA) 34
fixed assets 40
'flag' continuation patterns 82
FlexiSystems 5–13, 18
flipping of new issues 118
flotations *see* new issues
foreign exchange *see* forex
foreign language learning 16–17
foreign investing *see* international investing
forex 156–57
   Web sites 157, 192
forward rates 156
fraud *see* unscrupulous dealers
FSA (Financial Services Authority) 34
FTSE-100 stocks 29, 154
futures *see* financial futures

Gann, William 66
GDP *see* Gross Domestic Product
gearing 45, 96, 136
gearing ratio 45
Geo Interactive Media case study 46
global coordinators 110
'golden cross' signs 84
grey market prices 116
Gross Domestic Product (GDP), as inflationary indicator 51
growth companies, tip sheet coverage 126
growth investing, value investing compared 38–39
guaranteed stops 150
gurus 128–29

'head and shoulders' reversal pattern 82
hedging 137, 148
Hemmington Scott 126, 185
high-tech stocks 7, 54
   markets 26–27
   recommended reading 178
   Web sites 202
hours of trading 25

'ignorance cover-up' trick 165–66
'in the money' 135
income tax 104
inflationary indicators 51–52
infrastructure Internet companies 50
inheritance tax 105
Interactive Investor International *see* Ample
interest cover 96–97
interest rates 51–52
international investing 16–17
   foreign stock exchange Web sites 205–07
   general advice Web sites 205
   tip sheet coverage 127–28
Internet, advantages of 3–4
Internet companies 10, 49–51
   penny share category 93
   recommended reading 178
Internet service providers (ISPs) 27
intrinsic value 135
investment analysts 10–11, 53–55, 115
   Web sites 194–96
investment bank Web sites 54
investment clubs 12–13, 208
investment gurus 128–29
investment trusts 118
investor security 24
ISAs (Individual Savings Accounts) 32–33
ISPs (Internet service providers) 27

Jackson, Bruce 129

'keeping your capital' tricks 162–63
Kipling, Rudyard 70

languages, learning foreign 16–17
large-company information 54
lastminute.com 51, 114, 119–21
learning approach 2
Leeson, Nick 139–40
lemming effect 7–8

214 Index

level 11 data   22
liabilities, current and long-term   40
LIFFE (London International Financial Futures and Options Exchange)   136, 142, 155–56
limit orders   25, 29, 64, 150
line charts   77
liquidity checks   44–45
London International Financial Futures and Options Exchange see LIFFE
Long Term Capital Management (LTCM)   141
long-term liabilities   40
losses   68
LTCM (Long Term Capital Management)   141

macro-economic factors   51–52, 156–57
management quality factors   95–96
margin trading   26
market orders   25, 64
McWilliams, Bruce   95
media, complaining through the   34
medium-sized company information   54
Meriwether, John   141
message boards   129–30, 202–03
mobile Internet   22–23
modular design of book   1–2
money supply, as inflationary indicator   52
Motley Fool UK Web site   13–14
moving averages   83–84
Muirhead, Charles   95

naked Calls   138
Nasdaq   26–27, 113
NAV (net asset value) per share   43
Neff, John   176–77
net asset value (NAV) per share   43
net operating cash flow (NOCF)   47
net profit   40
neuro-linguistic programming (NLP)   69–70
new issues   25–26, 94, 109–21
　case study   119–21
　pricing and valuing   109–13
　researching   114–18
　selecting and applying for   113–14
　upon issue   118–19
　Web sites   116, 209
newsletters   87–88, 123, 124–28

free trial copies   125–27, 207
NLP (neuro-linguistic programming)   69–70
NMS (normal market size)   28–29
NOCF (net operating cash flow)   47
nominee accounts   30
normal market size (NMS)   28–29

OFEX (Off Exchange) trading facility   97–99
　Web sites   98, 204
O'Higgins method   44–45
on-the-move broking   22–23
'one-off sting' tricks   167–67
'one-sided case' tricks   163
one-stop financial shopping   26
O'Neil, William   74
online accounts, opening   28
online advantages of share trading   63–64
online bookshops   171–72, 209
online brokers see brokers, online
online education   15, 203
online services, advantages   3–4
Online Share Buyer's FlexiSystem   6–13, 18
options trading   133–42
　analysis   140–42
　recommended reading   176
　risk warnings   139–40
　Web sites   142, 198–99
Orange mobile phone company   119
Orchestream   95, 117
orders   25, 29
　share trading   64–65
'out of the money'   135
over-borrowing   45
overbought and oversold indicators   85–86
overseas investing see international investing

paper share certificates   30
paper trading see fantasy trading
Pareto's principle   68
'participating forwards'   138
passwords   24
PDAs (personal digital assistants)   22
PE (price/earnings) ratio   42
PEG ratio   43
'penetration of the trend'   80
penny shares   91–108
　buying and selling techniques   102

Index

categories 92–94
market manipulations 103
markets 97–101
selecting 94–97
tax advantages 103–05
tip sheet coverage 126
Web sites 105–06, 201–02
personal digital assistants (PDAs) 22
Personal Investment Authority (PIA) 33–34
point-and-figure charts 77
position trading 60
present value 47
price/earnings (PE) ratio 42
price/sales ratio (PSR) 49
pricing
  new issues 109–13
  obtaining stock prices 28–29
  options 141–42
primary trends 76
professionals, relying on 53–55
profit, trading options for 136–37
profit and loss accounts 39–40
Proshare 13
PSR (price/sales ratio) 49
pump-and-dump manoeuvres 167
Put–Call ratios 140–41
Put options 134–35, 137–38

'qualified recommendation' trick 161
qualitative factors 48–49
quick ratio 44

Random Walk theory 5
ratio analysis 38–39, 41–45
  recommended reading 176–77
reading recommendations 171–81
  online bookshops 171–72, 209
real option pricing 50
recovery stocks 92–93
rectangle continuation patterns 81–82
REFS services 38, 42, 46
reintracements 86–87
'relative strength' calculation 67
relative strength indicators 85–86
reports, annual 39–41
required rate of return 47
resistance levels, technical analysis charts 79
Retail Price Index (RPI), as inflationary indicator 52

return on capital employed (ROCE) 45
reversal patterns 82–83
rights issues 31
risk management 66
  of options 139–40
  of spread betting 150
Robert Walters recruitment agency 117
ROCE (return on capital employed) 45
Rotella, Robert P 62
RPI *see* Retail Price Index

'saucer top or bottom' pattern 83
Schultz, Harry D 127–28
Schwartz, Marty 74, 84
screener Web sites 55, 187
scrip issues 31–32
search engines, favourite 186
secondary market trading, and recent issues 119
secondary trends 76
Securities and Futures Authority (SFA) 33–34
security, investor 24
self-discipline 63
selling levels, setting 67
'selling short' 151
settlement arrangements 29–30
Seycota, Ed 65
SFA (Securities and Futures Authority) 33–34
share certificates 30
share price/NAV per share 43
'share price quote' Web sites 186–87
share tipping 123–31
share trading 59–71
  base for 62–63
  choosing brokers 64
  mistakes 61–62
  online advantages 63–64
  placing orders 64–65
  principles 65–66
  reading recommendations 174–75
  self-development 69–70
  self-discipline 63
  timing 66–68
  Web sites 69, 197–98
shareholders, rights of 31–34
shareholders' funds 40
Sharp, Dr Van K 62
sharp practice *see* unscrupulous dealers
shell companies 92–93

simulated (fantasy) training   25, 70
'size of company' factors   11
Slater, Jim   44, 126–27, 177
small company information   54
Sovereign Society   128
speculation   8, 150–51
spot rates   156
spread betting   148–53
   recommended reading   175–76
   Web sites   152–53, 189–90
spread trading   154
stochastics   86
stock exchange Web sites   186, 205–07
stock market news Web sites   196–97
stock screener Web sites   55, 187
stop losses   68, 102, 150
straddle trading strategy   138
strike prices   133–34, 135
support levels, technical analysis charts   79
swing trading   60
syndicate desks   114–15

T + 3 settlement   29
takeovers   32
'tarantulas'   139
targeted dubious stock promotions   166–67
taxation   32–33
   avoidance   128
   unquoted company investments   103–05
   Web sites   105, 204
TechMARK index   101, 205
technical analysis   73–89
   charts   76–83
   further reading and research   87–88, 175
   technical indicators   83–86
   theories   74–76, 86–87
   Web sites   88, 199–20
technical indicators   83–86
telecommunications, media and technology (TMT) stocks   7, 8
telephone back-up services   23
Temple, Peter   128
terminal value   47
tertiary trends   76
time value   135–36, 144
timing   9–10
   flotations   117
   share trading   66–68
tip sheets   125–28
   free trial copies   125–27, 207

tipping *see* share tipping
TMT (telecommunications, media and technology) stocks   7, 8
'top hat' spreads   139
traded options *see* options
trading *see* share trading
trading hours   25
'traditional' options   134
trailing stop losses   68
trends, on technical analysis charts   76, 79
   channels   79–80
   penetration   80
triangle continuation patterns   81
Turner, Toni   65

UFCs (universal futures contracts)   155–56
unconventional advice Web sites   207–08
unemployment figures, as inflationary indicator   52
universal futures contracts (UFCs)   155–56
unscrupulous dealers   103, 152–53, 161–69
   recommended reading   179
US markets   16, 101
   brokers and dealing facilities   26–27
   research information Web sites   54–55
US-style options   134

valuations of penny shares   94–95
value investing   5–13
   growth investing compared   38–39
   recommended reading   176–77
   tip sheet coverage   126–27
venture capital trusts (VCTs)   104–05, 116–17
Vintcent, Charles   150

WACC (weighted average cost of capital)   47–48
Walters, Michael   128–29
WAP (wireless application protocol) phones   22–23
WAP Web sites   208
warrants   118, 133, 143–44
   Web sites   144, 198
Watson, Stuart   60
Web site addresses, useful   185–209
   books that list   173
weighted average cost of capital (WACC)   47–48
wheeling and dealing   138
Winnifrith, Tom   126